150
BAKING
recipes
INSPIRED IDEAS FOR
EVERYDAY COOKING

150
CAKE
recipes
INSPIRED IDEAS FOR
EVERYDAY COOKING

150
CHICKEN
recipes

150
CUPCAKE
& MUFFIN
recipes
INSPIRED IDEAS FOR
EVERYDAY COOKING

150
FAST
& SIMPLE
recipes
INSPIRED IDEAS FOR
EVERYDAY COOKING

150
INDIAN
recipes
INSPIRED IDEAS FOR
EVERYDAY COOKING

150
PASTA
recipes
INSPIRED IDEAS FOR
EVERYDAY COOKING

150
SLOW
COOKER
recipes
INSPIRED IDEAS FOR
EVERYDAY COOKING

150
STIR-FRY
recipes
INSPIRED IDEAS FOR
EVERYDAY COOKING

150
STUDENT
recipes
INSPIRED IDEAS FOR
EVERYDAY COOKING

150
TAPAS
recipes
INSPIRED IDEAS FOR
EVERYDAY COOKING

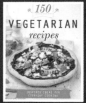

150
VEGETARIAN
recipes
INSPIRED IDEAS FOR
EVERYDAY COOKING

150

VEGETARIAN
recipes

INSPIRED IDEAS FOR
EVERYDAY COOKING

CONTENTS

INTRODUCTION 4
SOUPS & SALADS 6
QUICK & EASY 56
FAMILY FAVOURITES 106
SPECIAL OCCASIONS 156
DESSERTS 206
INDEX 254

INTRODUCTION

Whether you are a committed vegetarian or someone who prefers to eat less meat, fish and shellfish, this appetizing selection of vegetarian dishes is sure to inspire you in the kitchen. You'll find a vast choice of delicious and versatile vegetarian dishes to suit all tastes, featuring some sensational starters, snacks, main courses and desserts.

So, take your pick from this comprehensive collection of enticing recipes, packed full of flavour, colour, texture and appeal – you'll be amazed and delighted at just how creative and wide-ranging vegetarian dishes can be.

We begin with a chapter of wonderful warming soups and sensational salads. Tempt your taste buds with ever-popular favourites like Cream of Mushroom Soup, Leek & Potato Soup and Tomato,

Pasta Salad, or try something a bit different such as Celeriac Soup with Cheese Pastry Sticks, Roasted Root Soup with Ginger & Crème Fraîche, Broccoli Salad and Rainbow Salad with Wasabi Dressing.

Next, we feature some super quick and easy dishes, perfect for a speedy supper, lazy lunch or satisfying snack. This marvellous medley of fast and fabulous dishes ranges from pizzas, pasta and bruschetta to stir-fries, fritters and frittatas. Choose from tempting dishes like Melting Mozzarella Bagels, Beetroot & Roquefort Wraps and Wild Mushroom Omelette.

The next section on family favourites features an assortment of everyday homely dishes that includes comforting Macaroni Cheese or Spinach & Ricotta Cannelloni, satisfying Sweet Potato Curry with Lentils, tongue-tingling Vegetable Chilli and sophisticated Soufflé Jacket Potatoes or Sweet Potato Ravioli with Sage Butter. Or, why not try the wonderfully named Hoppin' John? It is sure to be a winner by its name alone!

This choice collection of vegetarian recipes wouldn't be complete without a chapter focusing on dishes designed for special occasions. So, prepare to impress your family and friends with our tempting range of recipes that will show off your creative flair in the kitchen. We feature tasty tarts such as Carrot Tarte Tatin or Caramelized Onion Tart and reliable rice dishes like Pumpkin & Chestnut Risotto or Vegetarian Paella. For nut-lovers, Jerusalem Artichoke & Hazelnut Gratin or Mixed Nut Roast with Cranberry & Red Wine Sauce will hit the spot, while Quinoa-stuffed Aubergines and Squash, Kale & Farro Stew make the most of some more unusual, but increasingly popular, nutritious grains.

Saving the best until last, satisfy your sweet tooth with our sensational selection of delicious desserts. We include some terrific sweet treats including pies, puddings, cobblers, cheesecakes and brûlées. All-time favourites such as Rice Pudding, Apple & Blackberry Crumble & Lemon Meringue Pie provide the perfect comfort pudding, or opt for choice chilled desserts like Eton Mess, Key Lime Pie, Red Wine Sorbet and Summer Pavlova. For committed chocoholics, Chocolate Mousse, Rich Chocolate Tarts and Chocolate Ice-cream Bites offer that all-important chocolate hit.

There are different types of vegetarian. The most common type, Lacto-ovo-vegetarians, don't eat red meat (including game), poultry, fish, shellfish or by-products of animal slaughter, but do eat dairy products and eggs. Lacto-vegetarians don't eat red meat (including game), poultry, fish, shellfish, by-products of animal slaughter or eggs, but do eat dairy products. Vegans don't eat red meat (including game), poultry, fish, shellfish, by-products of animal slaughter, dairy products, eggs or any other animal-derived products.

A typical vegetarian diet by its very nature can be a wholesome and nutritious way of eating. Choosing a wide variety of ingredients from different food groups every day (including vegetables, fruits, pulses, grains, nuts and seeds, plus dairy products and eggs – depending on the type of vegetarian diet) should provide vegetarians with a healthy and balanced diet that meets all their nutritional needs.

INTRODUCTION

SOUPS & SALADS

LEEK & SPINACH SOUP	8
CARROT & CORIANDER SOUP	10
CELERIAC SOUP WITH CHEESE PASTRY STICKS	12
TOMATO SOUP	14
SWEET POTATO & APPLE SOUP	16
CREAM OF MUSHROOM SOUP	18
BROCCOLI & STILTON SOUP	19
PEA & HERB SOUP WITH BASIL OIL	20
YELLOW TOMATO GAZPACHO	22
MUSHROOM & TOFU LAKSA WITH NOODLES	24
ROASTED ROOT SOUP WITH GINGER & CRÈME FRAÎCHE	26
LEEK & POTATO SOUP	28
CHUNKY VEGETABLE SOUP	29
WATERCRESS, COURGETTE & MINT SALAD	30
CARAMELIZED APPLE & BLUE CHEESE SALAD	31
PEAR, CELERY, BLUE CHEESE & WALNUT SALAD	32
BORLOTTI BEAN, TOMATO & ONION SALAD WITH EGGS	34
SPRING CABBAGE & RADISH SLAW WITH PUMPKIN SEEDS	36
CARROT, COCONUT & MANGO SALAD	38
GADO GADO SALAD	40
BROCCOLI SALAD	42
WARM BUTTERNUT SQUASH, MUSHROOM & SPINACH SALAD	44
CHUNKY AVOCADO & SWEETCORN SALAD	46
RAW BEETROOT & PECAN SALAD	47
POTATO & RADISH SALAD	48
RAINBOW SALAD WITH WASABI DRESSING	50
TOMATO, OLIVE & MOZZARELLA PASTA SALAD	52
RADICCHIO & RED PEPPER SALAD	54

LEEK & SPINACH SOUP

Serves: 4   **Prep: 20 mins**   **Cook: 45 mins**

Ingredients

25 g/1 oz butter

2 leeks, trimmed, halved lengthways and thinly sliced

225 g/8 oz potatoes, cut into bite-sized chunks

300 g/10½ oz spinach, stalks discarded, leaves sliced

300 ml/10 fl oz hot vegetable stock

1 tsp lemon juice

pinch of freshly grated nutmeg

sea salt and pepper

soured cream, to serve

Method

1 Melt the butter in a large saucepan over a medium–low heat. Add the leeks and potatoes, cover and gently cook for 10 minutes, or until beginning to soften.

2 Stir in two thirds of the spinach. Cover and cook for 2–3 minutes, until starting to wilt. Season with salt and pepper. Stir in half the stock. Bring to the boil, then simmer for 20 minutes, partially covered.

3 Transfer half the soup to a food processor and process until smooth. Return to the pan.

4 Purée the remaining uncooked spinach and the remaining stock. Add to the soup in the pan. Stir in the lemon juice and nutmeg and gently reheat.

5 Ladle into warmed bowls, swirl in a spoonful of soured cream and serve immediately.

★ Variation

Instead of using spinach, try nutritious kale.

CARROT & CORIANDER SOUP

Serves: 6

Prep: 15 mins, plus cooling

Cook: 45 mins

Ingredients

3 tbsp olive oil

1 red onion, chopped

1 large potato, chopped

1 stick celery, chopped

500 g/1 lb 2 oz carrots, chopped

1 litre/1¾ pints vegetable stock

1 tbsp butter

2 tsp coriander seeds, crushed

1½ tbsp chopped fresh coriander, plus extra to garnish

225 ml/8 fl oz milk

salt and pepper

Method

1 Heat the oil in a large saucepan. Add the onion and cook over a low heat, stirring occasionally, for 5 minutes, until softened.

2 Add the potato and celery and cook, stirring occasionally, for 5 minutes, then add the carrots and cook for a further 5 minutes. Cover the pan, reduce the heat to very low and cook, shaking the pan occasionally, for 10 minutes.

3 Pour in the stock and bring to the boil, then cover and simmer for 10 minutes, until the vegetables are tender.

4 Meanwhile, melt the butter in a frying pan. Add the coriander seeds and cook, stirring constantly, for 1 minute. Add the chopped coriander and cook, stirring constantly, for 1 minute, then remove from the heat.

5 Remove the soup from the heat and leave to cool slightly. Transfer to a food processor or blender, in batches if necessary, and process until smooth. Return the soup to the rinsed-out pan, stir in the coriander mixture and milk and season to taste with salt and pepper. Reheat gently, then serve, sprinkled with chopped coriander.

CELERIAC SOUP WITH CHEESE PASTRY STICKS

Serves: 4   **Prep: 35 mins**   **Cook: 40 mins**

Ingredients

3 tbsp olive oil

1 onion, chopped

1 celeriac, peeled and cut into chunks

1 litre/1¾ pints vegetable stock

1 small bunch fresh thyme, chopped

salt and pepper

fresh thyme sprigs, to garnish

Cheese sticks

375 g/13 oz ready-made puff pastry, thawed if frozen

plain flour, for dusting

1 egg, beaten

100 g/3½ oz finely grated vegetarian Parmesan-style cheese

butter, for greasing

pepper

Method

1 Heat the oil in a large saucepan over a medium heat, add the onion and cook, stirring frequently, for 4–5 minutes, until soft but not coloured.

2 Add the celeriac and cook, stirring frequently, for 3–4 minutes. Pour in the stock and add the thyme. Simmer for 25 minutes, or until the celeriac is tender. Meanwhile, preheat the oven to 200°C/400°F/Gas Mark 6.

3 To make the cheese sticks, thinly roll out the pastry on a floured work surface. Brush with half the egg, scatter over half the cheese and season well with pepper.

4 Fold the pastry in half. Brush with the remaining egg, scatter with the remaining cheese and season with pepper. Lightly grease and line two baking sheets.

5 Cut the pastry into strips about 1 cm/½ inch wide. Twist gently along their length to produce spirals. Place on the prepared baking sheets and bake in the preheated oven for 5 minutes, or until crisp and golden.

6 Purée the soup in the pan using a hand-held blender and gently reheat. Season to taste with salt and pepper.

7 Ladle the soup into warmed bowls, garnish with thyme sprigs and serve with the warm cheese pastry sticks.

TOMATO SOUP

Serves: 4 **Prep: 15 mins** **Cook: 35 mins**

Ingredients

25 g/1 oz butter

2 tbsp olive oil

1 large onion, finely chopped

2 garlic cloves, finely chopped

1 celery stick, finely chopped

500 g/1 lb 2 oz plum tomatoes, peeled, cored and chopped

2 tbsp tomato purée

100 ml/3½ fl oz water

brown sugar, to taste

1 tbsp chopped fresh basil, plus extra to garnish

300 ml/10 fl oz vegetable stock

salt and pepper

Method

1 Melt the butter with the oil in a saucepan. Add the onion, garlic and celery and cook over a low heat, stirring occasionally, for 5 minutes, until softened. Stir in the tomatoes, tomato purée and water. Increase the heat to medium and bring to the boil, then reduce the heat and simmer, stirring occasionally, for 10 minutes

2 Increase the heat to medium, then stir in sugar to taste, the basil and stock. Season to taste with salt and pepper. Bring to the boil, then reduce the heat and simmer for a further 10 minutes.

3 Taste and adjust the seasoning, adding salt and pepper if needed. Ladle into warmed bowls, garnish with basil and serve immediately.

SWEET POTATO & APPLE SOUP

Serves: 6 **Prep: 20 mins,** plus cooling **Cook: 50 mins**

Ingredients

1 tbsp butter

3 leeks, thinly sliced

1 large carrot, thinly sliced

600 g/1 lb 5 oz sweet potatoes, peeled and diced

2 large Bramley apples, peeled, cored and diced

1.2 litres/2 pints water

freshly grated nutmeg

225 ml/8 fl oz apple juice

225 ml/8 fl oz single cream

salt and pepper

snipped fresh chives or coriander, to garnish

Method

1 Melt the butter in a large saucepan over a medium–low heat.

2 Add the leeks, cover and cook for 6–8 minutes, or until soft, stirring frequently.

3 Add the carrot, sweet potatoes, apples and water. Lightly season to taste with salt, pepper and nutmeg. Bring to the boil, reduce the heat and simmer, covered, for about 20 minutes, stirring occasionally, until the vegetables are very tender.

4 Leave the soup to cool slightly, then purée in the pan with a hand-held blender.

5 Stir in the apple juice, place over a low heat and simmer for about 10 minutes, until heated through.

6 Stir in the cream and simmer for a further 5 minutes, stirring frequently, until heated through. Taste and adjust the seasoning, if necessary.

7 Ladle the soup into warmed bowls, garnish with chives and serve immediately.

CREAM OF MUSHROOM SOUP

Serves: 4

Prep: 15 mins,
plus cooling

Cook: 1 hour 40 mins–
1 hour 50 mins

Ingredients

115 g/4 oz unsalted butter

900 g/2 lb white button
mushrooms, thickly sliced

1 onion, roughly chopped

1 tbsp flour

1 litre/1¾ pints vegetable
stock

225 ml/8 fl oz water

6 sprigs fresh thyme, plus
picked leaves to garnish

3 cloves garlic

225 ml/8 fl oz double cream

salt and pepper

Method

1 Melt the butter in a large saucepan over a
medium heat. Add the mushrooms and
a pinch of salt. Cook, stirring occasionally, for
20–30 minutes, or until the mushrooms are
golden brown. Reserve some of the browned
mushrooms to garnish the soup later.

2 Add the onion and cook over a medium–low
heat for about 5 minutes. Add the flour and
cook, stirring, for 1 minute. Whisk in the stock
and water. Add the thyme and garlic, and
bring to a simmer. Reduce the heat to low,
cover, and simmer gently for 1 hour.

3 Remove the soup from the heat, uncover, and
allow to cool for 15 minutes. Transfer to a food
processor or blender, in batches if necessary,
and process until smooth.

4 Return the soup to the rinsed-out pan and gently
reheat; do not boil. Add the cream, taste and
adjust the seasoning, according to taste. Serve
hot, topped with the reserved mushrooms and
thyme leaves.

BROCCOLI & STILTON SOUP

Serves: 4-6 **Prep: 20 mins, plus cooling** **Cook: 40-45 mins**

Ingredients

40 g/1½ oz butter

2 onions, chopped

1 large potato, chopped

750 g/1 lb 10 oz broccoli florets

1.5 litres/2¾ pints vegetable stock

150 g/5½ oz vegetarian Stilton cheese, diced

pinch of ground mace

salt and pepper

ready-made croûtons, to garnish

Method

1 Melt the butter in a large saucepan. Add the onions and potato and stir well. Cover and cook over a low heat for 7 minutes. Add the broccoli and stir well, then re-cover the pan and cook for a further 5 minutes.

2 Increase the heat to medium, pour in the stock and bring to the boil. Reduce the heat, season to taste with salt and pepper and re-cover. Simmer for 15–20 minutes, until the vegetables are tender.

3 Remove the pan from the heat, strain into a bowl, reserving the vegetables, and leave to cool slightly. Put the vegetables into a food processor, add 1 ladleful of the stock and process to a smooth purée. With the motor running, gradually add the remaining stock.

4 Return the soup to the rinsed-out pan and reheat gently, but do not allow the soup to boil. Remove from the heat and stir in the cheese until melted and thoroughly combined. Stir in the mace and taste and adjust the seasoning, if necessary. Ladle into warmed serving bowls, sprinkle with the croûtons and serve.

SOUPS & SALADS

PEA & HERB SOUP WITH BASIL OIL

Serves: 4

Prep: 20 mins,
plus cooling

Cook: 25 mins

Ingredients

25 g/1 oz butter

6 spring onions, chopped

1 celery stick, finely chopped

375 g/13 oz frozen peas or fresh shelled peas

700 ml/1¼ pints vegetable stock

2 tbsp chopped fresh dill

1 tbsp snipped fresh chives

35 g/1¼ oz rocket leaves

2 tbsp crème fraîche

salt and pepper

bread sticks, to serve

Basil oil

1 x 25-g/1-oz bunch of basil

200 ml/7 fl oz olive oil

Method

1 Melt the butter in a saucepan over a medium heat. Add the spring onions and celery, cover and cook for 5 minutes until soft. Add the peas and stock, bring to the boil and simmer for 10 minutes. Remove from the heat. Cover and leave to cool for 20 minutes.

2 To make the basil oil, remove the stems from the basil and discard. Place the leaves in a food processor with half the oil and blend to a purée. Add the remaining oil and blend again. Transfer to a small bowl.

3 Add the dill, chives and rocket to the soup. Blend with a hand-held blender until smooth. Stir in the crème fraîche. If serving warm, heat through gently without boiling, then season to taste.

4 Ladle into four warmed bowls and drizzle with the basil oil. Serve immediately, with bread sticks on the side. If serving chilled, leave to cool completely, then chill in the refrigerator for at least 1 hour before checking the seasoning and serving.

YELLOW TOMATO GAZPACHO

Serves: 4–6

Prep: 30–35 mins, plus chilling

Cook: No cooking

Ingredients

900 g/2 lb large yellow tomatoes, halved

½ cucumber, peeled, deseeded and diced

1 yellow pepper, deseeded and diced

100 g/3½ oz red cherry tomatoes, deseeded and chopped

3 large spring onions, finely chopped

1–2 green chillies, deseeded and finely chopped

2 tbsp wine vinegar

3 tbsp extra virgin olive oil, plus extra for drizzling

4 garlic cloves

½ tbsp sea salt flakes, plus extra to taste

¼ tsp pepper, plus extra to taste

¼ tsp sugar

small handful basil leaves, shredded, to garnish

garlic ready-made croûtons, to serve

Method

1 Scoop out the seeds and juice from the yellow tomatoes. Pass the seeds and juice through a sieve set over a bowl. Chop the flesh and add to the bowl. Set aside 4 tablespoons each of the cucumber and yellow pepper. Set aside all of the chopped cherry tomatoes.

2 Add the remaining cucumber and yellow pepper to the yellow tomatoes. Add the onions, chilli, vinegar and oil. Tip into a food processor. Process, scraping down frequently, for 2 minutes, until very smooth. Pour back into the bowl.

3 Put the garlic into a mortar with the salt and crush with a pestle. Stir into the tomato mixture with the pepper and sugar. Chill for several hours until really cold.

4 Check the seasoning, adding more salt and pepper as necessary. Ladle into chilled soup plates or bowls. Top with the reserved yellow pepper, the cucumber and the cherry tomatoes. Add a slick of oil and a few shredded basil leaves and serve with garlic croûtons.

MUSHROOM & TOFU LAKSA WITH NOODLES

Serves: 4 **Prep: 25 mins** **Cook: 10–15 mins**

Ingredients

850 ml/1½ pints vegetable stock

400 g/14 oz canned coconut milk

250 g/9 oz shiitake mushrooms, stalks removed, thinly sliced

150 g/5½ oz firm tofu, cubed

2 tbsp tomato purée

175 g/6 oz fine egg noodles

salt and pepper

8 spring onions, sliced, and 4 tbsp shredded mint leaves, to garnish

Spice paste

2 red chillies, deseeded and chopped

4-cm/1½-inch piece fresh ginger, chopped

2 large garlic cloves, chopped

2 lemon grass stalks, tough outer layers discarded, inner stalks chopped

1 tsp coriander seeds, crushed

6 macadamia nuts, chopped

small handful of coriander leaves

3 tbsp vegetable oil

Method

1 Place the spice paste ingredients into a food processor or blender and process until smooth.

2 Heat a wok over a medium–high heat, add the spice paste and stir-fry for 30 seconds. Pour in the stock and coconut milk, and bring to the boil. Add the mushrooms, tofu and tomato purée and season with salt and pepper. Simmer gently for 5 minutes.

3 Cook the noodles in a saucepan of boiling water for 3–4 minutes, or cook according to the packet instructions, until tender. Divide between four large warmed soup bowls. Ladle the spicy broth over the noodles. Serve garnished with the spring onions and mint.

ROASTED ROOT SOUP WITH GINGER & CRÈME FRAÎCHE

Serves: 4–6   **Prep: 25 mins**   **Cook: 35–40 mins**

Ingredients

1 onion
½ small swede
1 sweet potato
2 carrots
1 potato
5 tbsp olive oil
2 tbsp tomato purée
¼ tsp pepper
2 large garlic cloves, peeled
2 tbsp groundnut oil
2 x 5-cm/2-inch pieces fresh ginger, sliced into thin shreds
850 ml/1½ pints hot vegetable stock
½ tsp sea salt
crème fraîche and roughly chopped fresh flat-leaf parsley, to garnish

Method

1 Preheat the oven to 190°C/375°F/Gas Mark 5. Peel the vegetables and cut into large, even-sized chunks. Mix the olive oil, tomato purée and pepper in a large bowl. Add the vegetables and the garlic and toss to coat.

2 Spread out the vegetables in a roasting tray. Roast in the preheated oven for 20 minutes, or until the garlic is soft. Remove the garlic and set aside. Roast the vegetables for a further 10–15 minutes, until tender.

3 Meanwhile, heat the groundnut oil in a frying pan over a high heat. Add the ginger and fry, turning constantly, for 1–2 minutes, until crisp. Immediately remove the ginger from the pan and drain on kitchen paper. Set aside and keep warm.

4 Put the garlic and the other roasted vegetables into a food processor. Process in short bursts to a rough-textured purée. Pour the purée into a saucepan and add the stock. Add the salt, then simmer, stirring, for 1–2 minutes, until heated through.

5 Ladle the soup into warmed serving bowls and swirl in a little crème fraîche. Top with the sizzled ginger threads and chopped parsley and serve immediately.

LEEK & POTATO SOUP

Serves: 6 **Prep: 15 mins** **Cook: 30 mins**

Ingredients

55 g/2 oz butter
1 onion, chopped
3 leeks, sliced
225 g/8 oz potatoes, cut into 2 cm/¾ inch cubes
850 ml/1½ pints vegetable stock
salt and pepper
150 ml/5 fl oz single cream, to serve
snipped fresh chives, to garnish

Method

1 Melt the butter in a large saucepan over a medium heat, add the onion, leeks and potatoes and sauté gently for 2–3 minutes, until soft but not brown. Pour in the stock, bring to the boil, then reduce the heat and simmer, covered, for 15 minutes.

2 Process using a hand-held blender, until smooth.

3 Heat the soup gently and season to taste with salt and pepper. Ladle into warmed bowls, garnish with a swirl of cream and snipped chives and serve immediately.

CHUNKY VEGETABLE SOUP

Serves: 4   **Prep: 15 mins**   **Cook: 20–25 mins**

Ingredients

1 red onion

1 stick celery

1 courgette

2 carrots

2 tbsp sunflower oil

400 g/14 oz canned
chopped plum tomatoes

300 ml/10 fl oz vegetable
stock

1 large sprig of fresh thyme

salt and pepper

chopped fresh thyme,
to garnish

Method

1 Cut the onion, celery, courgette and carrots into
1-cm/½-inch cubes.

2 Heat the oil in a large saucepan over a medium
heat. Add the vegetables and sauté, stirring, for
5 minutes without browning.

3 Add the tomatoes, stock and the thyme
sprig. Bring to the boil, then reduce the heat.
Cover and simmer for 10–15 minutes, until the
vegetables are just tender. Remove and
discard the thyme sprig and season to taste
with salt and pepper.

4 Transfer the soup to warmed serving bowls.
Garnish with chopped thyme and serve
immediately.

SOUPS & SALADS

WATERCRESS, COURGETTE & MINT SALAD

Serves: 4

Prep: 15 mins, plus cooling

Cook: 12 mins

Ingredients

2 courgettes, cut into batons

100 g/3½ oz French beans, cut into thirds

1 green pepper, deseeded and cut into strips

2 celery sticks, sliced

1 bunch watercress

salt

Dressing

200 ml/7 fl oz natural yogurt

1 garlic clove, crushed

2 tbsp chopped fresh mint

pepper

Method

1 Bring a saucepan of lightly salted water to the boil, add the courgette batons and beans, bring back to the boil and cook for 7–8 minutes.

2 Drain, rinse under cold running water and drain again. Set aside to cool completely.

3 Mix the courgettes and beans with the green pepper strips, celery and watercress in a large serving bowl.

4 To make the dressing, combine the yogurt, garlic and mint in a small bowl. Season to taste with pepper. Toss with the salad and serve immediately.

SOUPS & SALADS

CARAMELIZED APPLE & BLUE CHEESE SALAD

Serves: 2

Prep: 15 mins,
plus cooling

Cook: 6–7 mins

Ingredients

15 g/½ oz butter

2 tbsp sunflower oil or rapeseed oil

1 large red-skinned dessert apple, such as Pink Lady, cored and cut into thin wedges

2 tsp clear honey

1½ tsp fresh thyme leaves

1½ tbsp white wine vinegar

2 tsp wholegrain mustard

55g/2 oz mixed salad leaves

40 g/1½ oz vegetarian blue cheese, crumbled

25 g/1 oz walnuts, toasted and roughly chopped

2 tbsp snipped chives

salt and pepper

Method

1 Heat the butter with 1 teaspoon of the oil in a frying pan. Add the apples and fry for 2 minutes, stirring occasionally, until soft. Add the honey and thyme and continue to cook until the apples begin to caramelize. Remove from the heat.

2 Stir in the remaining oil, the vinegar and mustard. Season with pepper and a little salt and leave to cool slightly.

3 Place the salad leaves, cheese, walnuts and chives in a serving bowl. Spoon over the apples and warm dressing from the pan. Toss together and serve immediately.

SOUPS & SALADS

PEAR, CELERY, BLUE CHEESE & WALNUT SALAD

Serves: 4　　　　**Prep: 20–25 mins**　　　　**Cook: No cooking**

Ingredients

4 celery sticks

1 large, juicy red-skinned pear

lemon juice

3 tbsp chopped fresh flat-leaf parsley

150 g/5½ oz dark green salad leaves, such as rocket, watercress or baby spinach

100 g/3½ oz vegetarian blue cheese, broken into small chunks

4 tbsp roughly chopped walnuts

sea salt flakes

Dressing

1 large, juicy pear

1 tbsp lemon juice

4 tbsp walnut oil

¼ tsp pepper

sea salt flakes

Method

1 Trim the celery and remove the strings with a swivel peeler. Slice into bite-sized pieces. Put into a shallow bowl.

2 Quarter and core the pear but do not peel. Slice each quarter lengthways into thin segments. Add to the celery. Sprinkle with a little lemon juice to prevent discoloration.

3 To make the dressing, quarter and core the pear. Slice one quarter lengthways into thin segments. Add to the pears in the bowl. Peel and roughly chop the remaining pear quarters.

4 Process the chopped pear with the remaining dressing ingredients with a hand-held blender. Process for 30 seconds until very smooth. Scrape into a small bowl.

5 Toss the celery and pears with about 5 tablespoons of the dressing, or enough to just coat. Stir in the parsley. Season with a pinch of salt.

6 Arrange the salad leaves on individual plates. Pile the pear and celery mixture attractively on top. Sprinkle with the cheese and nuts.

7 Spoon the remaining dressing over the salad and serve immediately.

BORLOTTI BEAN, TOMATO & ONION SALAD WITH EGGS

Serves: 4

Prep: 25 mins,
plus soaking

**Cook: 1 hour 45 mins–
2 hours 15 mins**

Ingredients

250 g/9 oz dried borlotti beans, soaked in cold water for several hours

2 large garlic cloves, crushed

juice of 2 lemons

6 tbsp extra virgin olive oil

1 tsp salt

1 small onion, finely diced

2 tomatoes, deseeded and finely diced

about 40 g/1½ oz fresh flat-leaf parsley, thick stems removed, leaves chopped

1 tsp cumin seeds, crushed

pepper

warmed pitta breads, to serve

To garnish

4 hard-boiled eggs, quartered

4 lemon wedges

sumac or crushed red pepper flakes

Method

1 Drain the beans, rinse well and put into a large saucepan. Cover with water and bring to the boil. Boil for 10 minutes, then reduce the heat and simmer for 1½–2 hours, or until very tender. Top up with boiling water if necessary.

2 Drain the beans and tip into a shallow serving dish. Lightly crush some of them with the back of a wooden spoon.

3 Add the garlic, lemon juice, olive oil and salt while the beans are still warm. Mix gently, then add the onion, tomatoes and parsley. Add the cumin seeds and some pepper and gently toss.

4 Arrange the egg quarters and lemon wedges on top. Sprinkle with a pinch of sumac. Serve with fingers of warm pitta bread.

SPRING CABBAGE & RADISH SLAW WITH PUMPKIN SEEDS

Serves: 4–6

Prep: 20 mins, plus standing

Cook: No cooking

Ingredients

1 Hispi spring cabbage, or ¼ head white cabbage

10–15 radishes, trimmed and sliced

½ small red onion, thinly sliced

3 tbsp pumpkin seeds

small bunch dill, about 20 g/¾ oz, thick stems removed, leaves roughly sliced

2 small handfuls micro-leaves, such as radish sprouts

1 handful pea shoots

salt

Dressing

3 tbsp Greek-style yogurt

1 tbsp whipping cream

2 tsp extra virgin olive oil

¾ tsp Dijon mustard

good squeeze of lemon juice

Method

1 Discard any coarse outer leaves from the cabbage. Trim the base and cut the cabbage in quarters lengthways. Cut out the core and discard. Slice each quarter crossways into ribbons. Place in a colander set over a bowl and sprinkle with salt. Toss with your hands and leave to stand for 30 minutes.

2 To make the dressing, combine all the ingredients in a small bowl, mixing well.

3 Blot the cabbage with kitchen paper. Tip into a shallow serving dish. Add the radishes, onion, pumpkin seeds and dill.

4 Spoon over the dressing and toss to mix. Scatter the micro-leaves and pea shoots over the top of the slaw and serve.

CARROT, COCONUT & MANGO SALAD

Serves: 2–3

Prep: 25 mins, plus standing

Cook: No cooking

Ingredients

350 g/12 oz young carrots, scrubbed

1 ripe mango, about 375 g/13 oz, peeled and cut into small cubes

55 g/2 oz fresh coconut flesh, very thinly sliced

3 tbsp chopped fresh coriander

3 tbsp toasted skinned hazelnuts, roughly chopped

½ tsp muscovado sugar

½ tsp sea salt flakes

finely grated rind of 1 lime

lime segments, to garnish

Dressing

1 tsp muscovado sugar

¼ tsp sea salt

juice of 1 lime

¼–½ small green chilli, deseeded and very finely chopped

3 tbsp hazelnut oil or light olive oil

pepper

Method

1 Cut the carrots into 5-cm/2-inch lengths. Using a swivel peeler, shave into wide ribbons, discarding the woody core. Put into a shallow dish and add the mango and coconut.

2 To make the dressing, dissolve the sugar and salt in the lime juice. Stir in the chilli and add pepper to taste. Add the oil and whisk until smooth.

3 Pour the dressing over the carrot mixture, tossing well. Leave to stand at room temperature for 20 minutes to allow the flavours to develop.

4 Add the coriander and toss again. Mix the hazelnuts with the sugar, salt and lime rind.

5 Arrange the carrot mixture on individual serving plates and sprinkle with the nut mixture. Garnish with lime segments and serve immediately.

GADO GADO SALAD

Serves: 4

Prep: 25 mins,
plus cooling

Cook: 3-4 mins

Ingredients

250 g/9 oz cauliflower,
cored and
cut into small florets

115 g/4 oz broccoli,
destemmed
and cut into small florets

115 g/4 oz Savoy cabbage,
shredded

150 g/5½ oz ready-to-
eat beansprouts

300 g/10½ oz cucumber,
peeled, halved lengthways,
deseeded and thickly
sliced

1 red pepper, halved,
deseeded
and finely chopped

Dressing

2 tbsp groundnut oil

85 g/3 oz unsalted peanuts,
finely chopped

2 garlic cloves, finely
chopped

2 tbsp soy sauce

juice of 2 limes

½ red chilli, deseeded and
finely chopped

Method

1 Put the cauliflower, broccoli, cabbage,
beansprouts, cucumber and red pepper in a
salad bowl and toss gently together.

2 To make the dressing, heat 1 tablespoon of the
oil in a frying pan over a medium heat. Add the
peanuts and garlic and stir-fry for 2–3 minutes,
or until lightly browned. Remove from the heat
and stir in the soy sauce, lime juice, chilli and
remaining oil, then leave to cool.

3 When ready to eat, spoon the dressing over the
salad and toss gently together. Spoon into four
bowls, then serve immediately.

BROCCOLI SALAD

Serves: 4 **Prep: 20 mins** **Cook: 10–15 mins**

Ingredients

200 g/7 oz purple sprouting broccoli

250 g/9 oz red cabbage, shredded

115 g/4 oz cooked beetroot in natural juices (drained weight), drained and cut into matchsticks

2 tbsp dried cranberries

3 tbsp balsamic vinegar

Croûtons

2 tbsp olive oil

85 g/3 oz rustic wholegrain bread, torn into small pieces

1 tbsp sunflower seeds

1 tbsp flaxseeds (linseeds)

Method

1 Put the broccoli in the top of a steamer, cover and set over a saucepan of simmering water. Steam for 3–5 minutes, or until tender. Cool under cold running water, then cut the stems in half and the lower stems in half again lengthways, and transfer them to a salad bowl.

2 Add the red cabbage, beetroot and dried cranberries to the salad bowl.

3 To make the croûtons, heat the oil in a frying pan over a medium heat, add the bread and fry for 3–4 minutes, stirring, until just beginning to brown. Add the sunflower seeds and flaxseeds and cook for 2–3 minutes more, until lightly toasted.

4 Drizzle the balsamic vinegar over the salad and toss gently together. Sprinkle with the croûtons and seeds and serve immediately.

WARM BUTTERNUT SQUASH, MUSHROOM & SPINACH SALAD

Serves: 4   **Prep: 25 mins**   **Cook: 20–25 mins**

Ingredients

1 small butternut squash

5 tbsp olive oil

squeeze of lemon juice

2–3 Portobello mushrooms, thinly sliced

½ tsp coriander seeds, crushed

40 g/1½ oz unskinned almonds, halved lengthways

½ tbsp balsamic vinegar

juice of 1 small orange

4 handfuls baby spinach

2 tbsp snipped chives

sea salt flakes and pepper

Method

1 Slice the squash where the neck meets the bulbous end. Slice the neck lengthways into quarters. Slice the end lengthways in half. Remove the peel and seeds.

2 Slice the neck pieces lengthways into thin segments. Slice the end pieces crossways into thin semi-circles.

3 Heat the oil in a large frying pan over a medium–high heat. Add the squash in a single layer and fry, turning, for 5–7 minutes, until lightly browned. You will need to do this in batches.

4 Sprinkle with salt and pepper and lemon juice. Using a slotted spoon, transfer to a large sieve set over a bowl and leave to drain.

5 Add the mushrooms and coriander seeds to the pan and fry for 5 minutes. Season with salt and pepper and sprinkle with a little lemon juice. Add to the squash in the sieve.

6 Add the almonds to the oil remaining in the pan and cook, stirring, until brown. Remove from the pan and set aside.

7 Pour the drained juices from the vegetables into the pan. Stir in the vinegar, orange juice and a splash of water. Stir for a few seconds.

8 Arrange the spinach on serving plates and pile the squash and mushrooms on top.

9 Scatter over the almonds and chives, pour over the pan juices and serve while still warm.

CHUNKY AVOCADO & SWEETCORN SALAD

Serves: 4   **Prep: 20 mins**   **Cook: 5 mins**

Ingredients

200 g/7 oz frozen sweetcorn

1 large avocado, halved, pitted, peeled and cut into cubes

175 g/6 oz cherry tomatoes, cut into quarters

½ red onion, finely chopped

1 small green pepper, halved, deseeded and cut into small chunks

40 g/1½ oz kale, shredded

25 g/1 oz fresh coriander, roughly chopped

Dressing

finely grated rind and juice of 1 lime

2 tbsp olive oil

salt and pepper

Method

1 Put the sweetcorn in a saucepan of boiling water. Bring back to the boil, then simmer for 3 minutes. Drain into a colander, rinse with cold water, drain again, then transfer to a salad bowl.

2 To make the dressing, put the lime rind and juice and oil in a jam jar, season to taste with salt and pepper, screw on the lid and shake well.

3 Add the avocado, tomatoes, onion, green pepper, kale and coriander to the salad bowl. Drizzle over the dressing and toss together. Spoon into four bowls and serve immediately.

RAW BEETROOT & PECAN SALAD

Serves: 4　　　**Prep: 15–20 mins**　　　**Cook: No cooking**

Ingredients

175 g/6 oz fresh beetroot,
roughly grated

8 radishes, thinly sliced

2 spring onions,
finely chopped

25 g/1 oz pecan nuts,
roughly chopped

8 red chicory leaves or
Little Gem lettuce leaves

Dressing

2 tbsp extra virgin olive oil

1 tbsp balsamic vinegar

2 tsp creamed horseradish
sauce

salt and pepper

Method

1　Combine the beetroot, radishes, spring onions and pecans in a bowl and toss well to mix evenly.

2　Place all the dressing ingredients in a small bowl and whisk lightly with a fork. Season to taste with salt and pepper and pour over the vegetables in the bowl, tossing to coat evenly.

3　Arrange the chicory or lettuce leaves on a serving platter and spoon the salad over them.

4　Serve the salad cold on its own or as an accompaniment to main dishes.

SOUPS & SALADS

POTATO & RADISH SALAD

Serves: 4   **Prep: 20 mins,** plus standing   **Cook: 35 mins**

Ingredients

300 g/10½ oz new potatoes

200 g/7 oz small cauliflower florets

4 tbsp extra virgin olive oil, plus extra if needed

4½ tsp red wine vinegar, plus extra if needed

200 g/7 oz fine French beans, cut into bite-sized pieces

4 spring onions, finely chopped

1 radish, thinly sliced

85 g/3 oz baby spinach leaves

2 tbsp toasted pine nuts

2 tbsp raisins or sultanas

salt and pepper

radicchio leaves and ciabatta bread, to serve

Method

1 Bring two saucepans of lightly salted water to the boil. Add the potatoes to one pan, bring back to the boil and cook for 20–25 minutes, until tender. Add the cauliflower florets to the other pan, bring back to the boil and cook for 5 minutes, or until tender-crisp.

2 Meanwhile, whisk together the oil, vinegar, and salt and pepper to taste in a serving bowl.

3 Use a large slotted spoon to remove the cauliflower florets from the pan, shaking off the excess water, and stir them into the dressing in the bowl.

4 Drop the beans into the cauliflower cooking water, bring back to the boil and cook for 5 minutes, or until tender-crisp. Drain well, then stir into the serving bowl.

5 Drain the potatoes and cool slightly under cold running water. Peel and cut into bite-sized pieces, then stir into the dressing together with the spring onions and radish. Make sure all the vegetables are coated with dressing, then set aside for at least 1 hour.

6 When ready to serve, line a platter with radicchio leaves. Stir the spinach into the serving bowl and add extra oil, vinegar and salt and pepper, if desired. Stir in the pine nuts and raisins.

7 Spoon the salad onto the radicchio leaves, adding any dressing left in the bowl. Serve with plenty of ciabatta bread to mop up the dressing.

RAINBOW SALAD
WITH WASABI DRESSING

Serves: 4

Prep: 15 mins,
plus cooling

Cook: 3–4 mins

Ingredients

1 tbsp sunflower oil

4 tbsp sunflower seeds

2 tbsp soy sauce

200 g/7 oz rainbow chard
leaves, shredded
and cut into strips

Dressing

1 tsp wasabi paste

1 tbsp mirin

juice of 1 small orange

pepper

Method

1 Heat the oil in a lidded frying pan over a
medium heat. Add the sunflower seeds, cover
with the lid and fry for 2–3 minutes, shaking the
pan so they don't stick, until you hear them
begin to pop. Remove the pan from the heat,
add the soy sauce, cover with the lid again and
leave to cool.

2 To make the dressing, put the wasabi paste, mirin
and orange juice in a jam jar, season with a little
pepper, screw on the lid and shake well.

3 Put the chard leaves in a salad bowl. Drizzle over
the dressing then toss gently together. Sprinkle on
the toasted sunflower seeds and serve.

TOMATO, OLIVE & MOZZARELLA PASTA SALAD

Serves: 4

Prep: 15 mins, plus cooling

Cook: 15 mins

Ingredients

225 g/8 oz dried conchiglie

50 g/1¾ oz pine nuts

350 g/12 oz cherry tomatoes, halved

1 red pepper, deseeded and cut into bite-size chunks

1 red onion, chopped

200 g/7 oz vegetarian mozzarella di bufala, cut into small pieces

12 black olives, stoned

25 g/1 oz fresh basil leaves

Parmesan-style vegetarian cheese shavings, to garnish

salt

Dressing

5 tbsp extra virgin olive oil

2 tbsp balsamic vinegar

1 tbsp chopped fresh basil

salt and pepper

Method

1 Bring a large saucepan of lightly salted water to the boil. Add the pasta, bring back to the boil and cook for 8–10 minutes, until tender but still firm to the bite. Drain thoroughly and leave to cool.

2 Meanwhile, heat a dry frying pan over a low heat, add the pine nuts, and cook, shaking the pan frequently, for 1–2 minutes until lightly toasted. Remove from the heat, transfer to a dish and leave to cool.

3 To make the dressing, put all the ingredients in a small bowl and mix together well. Cover with clingfilm and set aside.

4 Divide the pasta among four serving bowls. Add the pine nuts, tomatoes, pepper, onion, mozzarella and olives to each bowl. Sprinkle over the basil, then drizzle over the dressing. Garnish with Parmesan-style vegetarian cheese shavings and serve.

RADICCHIO & RED PEPPER SALAD

Serves: 4   **Prep: 15 mins**   **Cook: No cooking**

Ingredients

2 red peppers

1 head of radicchio, separated into leaves

4 cooked whole beetroots, cut into matchsticks

12 radishes, sliced

4 spring onions, finely chopped

4 tbsp ready-made vegetarian salad dressing

crusty bread, to serve

Method

1 Core and deseed the red peppers and cut into rounds.

2 Arrange the radicchio leaves in a salad bowl. Add the peppers, beetroots, radishes and spring onions.

3 Drizzle with the dressing, toss well and serve with crusty bread.

★ Variation

You can use ready-made salad dressing for speedy salads but if you have time make your own. For a simple dressing mix together the juice of ½ a lemon, 3 tablespoons of olive oil and 1 tablespoon Dijon mustard.

NEW POTATO, ROSEMARY & ROCKET PIZZA	58
CARROT & ORANGE STIR-FRY	60
POACHED EGGS 'FLORENTINE' WITH SPINACH & CHEDDAR	62
PASTA PESTO	64
ASPARAGUS & PEA FRITTATA	66
MUSHROOMS & SIZZLED SAGE ON SOURDOUGH TOAST	68
STUFFED TOMATOES	69
FETTUCCINE WITH TOMATO & MUSHROOM SAUCE	70
BRUSCHETTA WITH BROAD BEANS, MINT & GOAT'S CHEESE	72
LEEK & GOAT'S CHEESE TARTLETS	74
MUSHROOM STROGANOFF	76
MELTING MOZZARELLA BAGELS	78
LEEK & GOAT'S CHEESE CRÊPES	79
BEETROOT & ROQUEFORT WRAPS	80
COUSCOUS WITH ROAST CHERRY TOMATOES & PINE NUTS	81
GRILLED AUBERGINES WITH RED PEPPER, FETA & MINT	82
EASY RICE & PEAS	84
PORTOBELLO MUSHROOM BURGERS WITH MOZZARELLA	86
WILD MUSHROOM OMELETTE	88
CLASSIC STIR-FRIED VEGETABLES	90
FALAFEL BURGERS	92
KALE STIR-FRY	94
TOFU PARCELS	96
CHILLI BROCCOLI PASTA	98
CAULIFLOWER CHEESE	100
BROCCOLI WITH PEANUTS	102
EGGS WITH FRIED TOMATO, ONION & PEPPERS	103
SPAGHETTI OLIO E AGLIO	104

NEW POTATO, ROSEMARY & ROCKET PIZZA

Serves: 4   **Prep: 15 mins**   **Cook: 25 mins**

Ingredients

280 g/10 oz small waxy potatoes, unpeeled

2 tbsp olive oil, plus extra for greasing

2 garlic cloves, thinly sliced

1½ tbsp chopped fresh rosemary leaves

1 ready-made 30-cm/ 12-inch pizza base

85 g/3 oz vegetarian smoked cheese, coarsely grated

115 g/4 oz vegetarian Gruyère cheese, coarsely grated

8 Kalamata olives, stoned and halved

handful of rocket

sea salt and pepper

Method

1 Preheat the oven to 240°C/475°F/Gas Mark 9. Bring a saucepan of lightly salted water to the boil. Add the potatoes, bring back to the boil and blanch for 3 minutes. Drain, then thinly slice.

2 Heat the oil in a large frying pan over a medium–high heat. Add the potatoes and fry for 3–4 minutes, until lightly browned. Add the garlic, 1 tablespoon of the rosemary, and salt and pepper to taste. Fry for a further 1 minute.

3 Place the pizza base on a baking sheet. Sprinkle with two thirds of the smoked cheese and the Gruyère cheese. Arrange the potatoes on top. Add the remaining cheese, the olives and the remaining rosemary.

4 Bake in the preheated oven for 10 minutes, until lightly browned. Scatter over the rocket and serve immediately.

★ **Variation**

Add some green pepper slices with the olives and rosemary for extra taste.

QUICK & EASY

CARROT & ORANGE STIR-FRY

Serves: 4   **Prep: 15 mins**   **Cook: 10 mins**

Ingredients

2 tbsp sunflower oil

450 g/1 lb carrots, grated

225 g/8 oz leeks, shredded

2 oranges, peeled and segmented

2 tbsp tomato ketchup

1 tbsp demerara sugar

2 tbsp light soy sauce

100 g/3½ oz peanuts, chopped

Method

1 Heat the oil in a large wok. Add the carrots and leeks to the wok and stir-fry for 2–3 minutes, or until the vegetables are just soft.

2 Add the oranges to the wok and heat through gently, ensuring that you do not break up the orange segments as you stir the mixture.

3 Mix the ketchup, sugar and soy sauce together in a small bowl.

4 Add the ketchup mixture to the wok and stir-fry for a further 2 minutes.

5 Transfer the stir-fry to warmed serving bowls and scatter over the peanuts. Serve immediately.

POACHED EGGS 'FLORENTINE' WITH SPINACH & CHEDDAR

Serves: 4   **Prep: 15 mins**   **Cook: 13–15 mins**

Ingredients

1 tbsp olive oil

200 g/7 oz young spinach leaves

4 thick slices ciabatta bread

25 g/1 oz butter

4 large eggs

100 g/3½ oz vegetarian Cheddar cheese, grated

salt and pepper

freshly grated nutmeg, to serve

Method

1 Preheat the grill to high. Heat the oil in a wok or large saucepan, add the spinach and stir-fry for 2–3 minutes until the leaves are wilted. Drain in a colander, season to taste with salt and pepper and keep warm.

2 Toast the bread on both sides until golden. Spread one side of each slice with butter and place buttered side up in a baking sheet.

3 Bring a small saucepan of lightly salted water to the boil, crack the eggs into the water and poach for about 3 minutes until the whites are set but the yolks still runny. Remove from the pan with a draining spoon.

4 Arrange the spinach on the toast and top each slice with a poached egg. Sprinkle with the grated cheese. Cook under the preheated grill for 1–2 minutes until the cheese has melted. Sprinkle with nutmeg and serve immediately.

PASTA PESTO

Serves: 4   **Prep: 15 mins**   **Cook: 15 mins**

Ingredients

450 g/1 lb dried tagliatelle

salt

Pesto

2 garlic cloves

25 g/1 oz pine nuts

115 g/4 oz fresh basil leaves, plus extra to garnish

125 ml/4 fl oz olive oil

55 g/2 oz freshly grated vegetarian Parmesan-style cheese

Method

1 To make the pesto, put the garlic, pine nuts and a pinch of salt into a food processor and process briefly. Add the basil and process to a paste.

2 With the motor still running, gradually add the oil. Scrape into a bowl and beat in the cheese. Season to taste with salt.

3 Bring a large, heavy-based saucepan of lightly salted water to the boil. Add the tagliatelle, bring back to the boil and cook for 8–10 minutes, until tender but still firm to the bite.

4 Drain well, return to the saucepan and toss with half the pesto. Divide among warm serving dishes and top with the remaining pesto. Garnish with basil and serve immediately.

ASPARAGUS & PEA FRITTATA

Serves: 4   **Prep: 15 mins**   **Cook: 20–25 mins**

Ingredients

8 asparagus spears
350 g/12 oz peas, shelled
8 eggs
½ tsp sea salt
1 tbsp olive oil
large knob of butter
8 spring onions, trimmed and finely sliced
pepper
green salad, to serve

Method

1 Snap the woody ends from the asparagus and discard. Chop the stems into 1-cm/½-inch pieces and chop the tips into 2.5-cm/1-inch pieces.

2 Put the asparagus and peas into a steamer basket set over a saucepan of boiling water. Steam for 3 minutes. Remove from the heat and reserve.

3 Beat the eggs well. Add the salt and some pepper.

4 Heat the oil and butter in a 24-cm/9½-inch non-stick frying pan over a medium heat. Add the spring onions and fry for 2 minutes. Stir in the peas and asparagus. Pour in the eggs, stirring to distribute the vegetables evenly.

5 Cover the pan and cook over a medium–low heat for 10–12 minutes, or until the eggs are almost set. Place under a hot grill and cook for a further 3–5 minutes, or until the top is set. Turn out onto a serving plate and cut into wedges. Serve hot or warm with a green salad.

QUICK & EASY

MUSHROOMS & SIZZLED SAGE ON SOURDOUGH TOAST

Serves: 4   **Prep: 15 mins**   **Cook: 10 mins**

Ingredients

5 tbsp olive oil

2 tbsp roughly chopped fresh sage, plus 16–20 whole small leaves

400 g/14 oz even-sized chestnut mushrooms, halved

lemon juice

1 large garlic clove, thinly sliced

2 tbsp chopped fresh flat-leaf parsley

¼ tsp pepper

4 slices sourdough bread

sea salt flakes

vegetarian Parmesan-style cheese shavings, to garnish

Method

1 Heat the oil in a large frying pan over a medium–high heat. Add the chopped sage and sizzle for a few seconds. Add the mushrooms and fry for 3–4 minutes, until they are beginning to release their juices.

2 Add a squeeze of lemon juice, then add the garlic, parsley, pepper and a pinch of salt. Cook for a further 5 minutes.

3 Meanwhile, toast the bread on both sides. Place on warmed plates and pile the mushrooms on top. Sizzle the whole sage leaves in the oil remaining in the pan over a high heat for a few seconds, until crisp. Scatter over the mushrooms. Sprinkle over some cheese shavings and serve immediately.

QUICK & EASY

STUFFED TOMATOES

Serves: 4   **Prep: 15–20 mins**   **Cook: 15–20 mins**

Ingredients

4 beef tomatoes

300 g/10½ oz cooked rice

8 spring onions, chopped

3 tbsp chopped fresh mint

2 tbsp chopped
fresh flat-leaf parsley

3 tbsp pine nuts

3 tbsp raisins

2 tsp olive oil

salt and pepper

Method

1 Cut the tomatoes in half, then scoop out the seeds and discard.

2 Stand the tomatoes upside down on kitchen paper for a few moments in order for the juices to drain out.

3 Preheat the oven to 190°C/375°F/Gas Mark 5. Turn the tomatoes the right way up and sprinkle the insides with salt and pepper.

4 Mix together the rice, spring onions, mint, parsley, pine nuts and raisins in a bowl. Spoon the mixture into the tomato cups.

5 Drizzle over a little olive oil, then arrange the tomatoes on a baking sheet or baking dish. Cook in the preheated oven for 15–20 minutes, or until they are tender and cooked through.

6 Transfer the tomatoes to warmed serving plates and serve immediately.

QUICK & EASY

FETTUCCINE WITH TOMATO & MUSHROOM SAUCE

Serves: 4   **Prep: 15 mins**   **Cook: 25–30 mins**

Ingredients

450 g/1 lb dried fettuccine

15 g/½ oz butter

2 tbsp grated vegetarian Parmesan-style cheese

salt

Tomato & mushroom sauce

25 g/1 oz butter

2 tbsp olive oil

1 large onion, finely chopped

2 garlic cloves, finely chopped

1 celery stick, finely chopped

400 g/14 oz canned chopped tomatoes

2 tbsp tomato purée

4 tbsp vegetarian dry red wine

115 g/4 oz mushrooms, sliced

brown sugar, to taste

1 tbsp chopped fresh basil

salt and pepper

Method

1 First, make the sauce. Melt the butter with the oil in a saucepan. Add the onion, garlic and celery and cook over a low heat, stirring occasionally, for 5 minutes, until softened. Stir in the tomatoes, tomato purée, wine and mushrooms. Increase the heat to medium and bring to the boil, then reduce the heat and simmer, stirring occasionally, for 15–20 minutes, until thickened.

2 Meanwhile, bring a large saucepan of lightly salted water to the boil. Add the fettuccine, bring back to the boil and cook for 8–10 minutes, until tender but still firm to the bite. Drain, tip into a warmed serving dish and toss with the butter.

3 Stir sugar to taste and the basil into the sauce and season to taste with salt and pepper. Pour the sauce over the pasta, toss well and sprinkle with the cheese. Serve immediately.

BRUSCHETTA WITH BROAD BEANS, MINT & GOAT'S CHEESE

Serves: 6   **Prep: 25 mins**   **Cook: 10 mins**

Ingredients

600 g/1 lb 5 oz shelled small broad beans (about 2.5 kg/5 lb 8 oz unshelled weight)

3 tbsp extra virgin olive oil, plus extra for drizzling

1 tbsp lemon juice

1 tbsp chopped fresh mint leaves

6 slices ciabatta

1 large garlic clove, halved

6 tbsp soft, fresh vegetarian goat's cheese

sea salt flakes and pepper

Method

1 Bring a large saucepan of lightly salted water to the boil. Add the beans, bring back to the boil and cook for 3 minutes, until just tender. Rinse under cold running water and drain.

2 Slip off the bean skins and discard.

3 Toss the beans with the oil, lemon juice and most of the mint. Season with a little salt and pepper.

4 Tip the bean mixture into a food processor. Process briefly to a chunky purée.

5 Toast the bread on both sides. While the bread is still warm, rub one side of each slice with the cut garlic clove. Drizzle with oil.

6 Cut each bread slice in half. Spread with the bean mixture, top with a little goat's cheese and the remaining mint.

QUICK & EASY

LEEK & GOAT'S CHEESE TARTLETS

Serves: 6   **Prep: 20 mins**   **Cook: 20 mins**

Ingredients

375 g/13 oz (1 rectangular sheet, 35 x 23 cm/ 14 x 9 inches) ready-rolled puff pastry

40 g/1½ oz butter

350 g/12 oz baby leeks, thickly sliced diagonally

1 tbsp chopped fresh oregano

125 g/4½ oz vegetarian goat's cheese, sliced or crumbled

milk, for brushing

salt and pepper

Method

1 Preheat the oven to 220°C/425°F/Gas Mark 7. Cut the pastry into six 12-cm/4½-inch squares.

2 Place the pastry squares on a baking sheet and use the tip of a sharp knife to score each one about 1-cm/½-inch from the edge all around.

3 Melt the butter in a frying pan, add the leeks and fry gently, stirring frequently, for 4–5 minutes until soft. Add the oregano, season with salt and pepper and divide the leek mixture between the pastry squares, placing it inside the scored lines.

4 Top each tartlet with cheese and brush the pastry with milk. Bake in the preheated oven for 12–15 minutes until risen and golden brown. Serve warm.

MUSHROOM STROGANOFF

Serves: 4   **Prep: 15 mins**   **Cook: 15–20 mins**

Ingredients

25 g/1 oz butter

1 onion, finely chopped

450 g/1 lb closed-cup mushrooms, quartered

1 tsp tomato purée

1 tsp wholegrain mustard

150 ml/5 fl oz crème fraîche

1 tsp paprika, plus extra to garnish

salt and pepper

fresh flat-leaf parsley sprigs, to garnish

Method

1 Heat the butter in a large, heavy-based frying pan. Add the onion and cook gently for 5–10 minutes until soft.

2 Add the mushrooms to the frying pan and stir-fry for a few minutes until they begin to soften.

3 Stir in the tomato purée and mustard, then add the crème fraîche. Cook gently, stirring constantly, for 5 minutes.

4 Stir in the paprika and season to taste with salt and pepper. Garnish with extra paprika and parsley sprigs and serve immediately.

MELTING MOZZARELLA BAGELS

Serves: 4 **Prep: 15–20 mins** **Cook: 20 mins**

Ingredients

½ aubergine, thinly sliced

3–4 tbsp olive oil

4 onion bagels or plain bagels

175 g/6 oz vegetarian mozzarella cheese, sliced

1 beef tomato, thinly sliced

salt and pepper

6–8 fresh basil leaves, torn in half if large, to serve

Method

1 Preheat a griddle pan until smoking. Brush the aubergine slices with a little of the oil, place on the pan and cook for 2 minutes on each side until tender and lightly charred.

2 Preheat the oven to 190°C/375°F/Gas Mark 5. Split the bagels in half and drizzle the cut sides with the remaining oil. Divide the cheese slices between the bagel bases and arrange the slices of tomato and aubergine on top. Season with salt and pepper and replace the bagel tops.

3 Place on a baking tray and bake in the preheated oven for 15 minutes until the cheese has melted and the bagels are beginning to toast around the edges. Add a few fresh basil leaves to each bagel and serve immediately.

QUICK & EASY

LEEK & GOAT'S CHEESE CRÊPES

Serves: 8   **Prep: 20 mins**   **Cook: 15 mins**

Ingredients

25 g/1 oz unsalted butter

½ tbsp sunflower oil

200 g/7 oz leeks, halved lengthways, rinsed and finely shredded

freshly grated nutmeg, to taste

1 tbsp finely snipped fresh chives

8 ready-made savoury crêpes

85 g/3 oz vegetarian soft goat's cheese, rind removed if necessary, chopped

salt and pepper

Method

1 Preheat the oven to 200°C/400°F/Gas Mark 6. Melt the butter with the oil in a heavy-based saucepan with a lid, uncovered over a medium–high heat. Add the leeks and stir until well coated. Stir in salt and pepper to taste.

2 Add a few gratings of nutmeg, then cover the leeks with a sheet of wet greaseproof paper and cover the pan. Reduce the heat to very low and leave the leeks to sweat for 5–7 minutes until very tender, but not brown. Stir in the chives, then taste and adjust the seasoning if necessary.

3 Put one crêpe on the work surface and put one eighth of the leeks on the crêpe, top with one eighth of the cheese.

4 Fold the crêpe into a square parcel or simply roll it around the filling. Place the stuffed crêpe on a baking tray, then continue to fill and fold or roll the remaining crêpes. Bake in the preheated oven for 5 minutes, or until the crêpes are hot and the cheese starts to melt.

QUICK & EASY

BEETROOT & ROQUEFORT WRAPS

Serves: 4　　　　**Prep: 15 mins**　　　　**Cook: 5 mins**

Ingredients

280 g/10 oz cooked
beetroot, diced

100 g/3½ oz
vegetarian Roquefort
cheese, crumbled

100 g/3½ oz walnuts, halved

1 tbsp mayonnaise

55 g/2 oz rocket

4 x 25-cm/10-inch multigrain
wraps

pepper

Method

1 Mix the beetroot, Roquefort, walnuts, and
mayonnaise together. Season with pepper to taste
and gently add the rocket leaves.

2 Preheat a non-stick pan or grill pan until almost
smoking, then cook the wraps one at a time
on both sides for 10 seconds. This will add some
colour and also soften the wraps.

3 Divide the mixture between the wraps,
placing in the middle of each wrap, and then
fold at the ends. Roll up, cut in half and
serve immediately.

QUICK & EASY

COUSCOUS WITH ROAST CHERRY TOMATOES & PINE NUTS

Serves: 4 **Prep: 15 mins** **Cook: 7–8 mins, plus standing**

Ingredients

300 g/10½ oz cherry tomatoes

3 tbsp olive oil

125 g/4½ oz couscous

200 ml/7 fl oz boiling water

25 g/1 oz pine nuts, toasted

5 tbsp roughly chopped fresh mint

finely grated rind of 1 lemon

½ tbsp lemon juice

salt and pepper

crisp green salad and vegetarian feta cheese, to serve

Method

1 Preheat the oven to 220°C/425°F/Gas Mark 7. Place the tomatoes and 1 tablespoon of the oil in a ovenproof dish. Toss together, then roast for 7–8 minutes in the preheated oven until the tomatoes are soft and the skins have burst. Leave to stand for 5 minutes.

2 Put the couscous in a heatproof bowl. Pour over the boiling water, cover and leave to stand for 8–10 minutes, until soft and the liquid has been absorbed.

3 Fluff up the couscous with a fork.

4 Add the tomatoes and their juices, the pine nuts, mint, lemon rind, lemon juice and the remaining oil. Season with salt and pepper, then gently toss together. Serve the couscous warm or cold, with a green salad and some feta cheese.

QUICK & EASY

GRILLED AUBERGINES WITH RED PEPPER, FETA & MINT

Serves: 4

Prep: 20 mins,
plus cooling/standing

Cook: 20 mins

Ingredients

1 red pepper, halved and deseeded

2 large firm aubergines, sliced crossways into 2-cm/¾-inch slices

olive oil, for brushing

2 garlic cloves, crushed

juice of 1 lemon

1½ tsp cumin seeds, crushed

50 g/1¾ oz vegetarian feta cheese, crumbled

2 tbsp roughly chopped fresh mint leaves

sea salt flakes and pepper

Method

1 Preheat the grill to high. Put the red pepper halves cut-side down on a roasting tray. Place under a very hot grill for about 10 minutes, or until the skin is black and blistered.

2 Remove from the heat and cover with a clean tea towel. Leave for 10 minutes to loosen the skin. Peel off the skin and cut the flesh into 5-mm/ ¼-inch dice.

3 Preheat a ridged griddle pan over a high heat. Brush the aubergine slices with oil on both sides and place in the pan, in batches, if necessary. Cook for about 2 minutes on each side, until grill marks appear.

4 Carefully remove the aubergine slices from the pan. Cut the larger slices in half.

5 In a large bowl, combine the garlic, red pepper, lemon juice and cumin. Season with salt and pepper.

6 Add the aubergine slices, turning carefully to coat, then arrange on a serving platter. Scatter over the cheese and mint leaves and serve at room temperature.

QUICK & EASY

EASY RICE & PEAS

Serves: 4   **Prep: 10 mins**   **Cook: 25–30 mins**

Ingredients

2 tbsp olive oil

1 onion, sliced

1 garlic clove, crushed

1 tbsp chopped thyme

400 ml/14 fl oz vegetable stock

200 g/7 oz basmati rice

4 tbsp coconut milk

400 g/14 oz canned red kidney beans, drained and rinsed

salt and pepper

fresh thyme sprigs, to garnish

Method

1 Heat the oil in a large saucepan, add the onion and fry over a medium heat, stirring, for about 5 minutes until soft.

2 Add the garlic and thyme and stir-fry for 30 seconds. Stir the stock into the pan and bring to the boil.

3 Stir in the rice, then reduce the heat, cover and simmer for 12–15 minutes, until the rice is just tender.

4 Stir in the coconut milk and beans, then season to taste with salt and pepper.

5 Cook gently for 2–3 minutes, stirring occasionally, until thoroughly heated. Serve hot, garnished with thyme.

PORTOBELLO MUSHROOM BURGERS WITH MOZZARELLA

Serves: 4   **Prep: 20 mins**   **Cook: 6–10 mins**

Ingredients

4 tsp olive oil

2 tsp red wine vinegar

1 garlic clove, finely chopped

4 large Portobello mushrooms, caps only

4–8 slices fresh vegetarian mozzarella cheese

4 x 15-cm/6-inch square pieces focaccia, split in half

50 ml/2 fl oz vegetarian pesto

tomato slices

baby rocket leaves

salt and pepper

Method

1 Preheat the grill to high and the oven to 160°C/325°F/Gas Mark 3. Whisk together the oil, vinegar and garlic in a medium-sized bowl. Place the mushrooms gill side-up on a baking tray, then drizzle with the vinaigrette and season to taste with salt and pepper.

2 Place under the preheated grill and cook for about 5–8 minutes until the mushrooms are tender. Place the cheese slices on top and cook for a further 1–2 minutes until bubbling. Meanwhile, put the focaccia on a lower rack in the preheated oven for 5 minutes to warm through.

3 Lightly spread the focaccia with the pesto, then add the mushrooms. Top with the tomato slices and rocket and serve immediately.

QUICK & EASY

WILD MUSHROOM OMELETTE

Serves: 2 **Prep: 20 mins** **Cook: 14–18 mins**

Ingredients

1 tsp extra virgin olive oil

1 small onion, cut into wedges

2–3 garlic cloves, crushed

85 g/3 oz mixed wild mushrooms, halved if large

85 g/3 oz closed-cup mushrooms, sliced

1 courgette, grated

2 eggs

2 egg whites

2 tbsp water

1 yellow pepper, deseeded and cut into strips

1 tbsp grated vegetarian Parmesan-style cheese (optional)

1 tbsp shredded fresh basil

salt and pepper

rocket, to garnish

wholemeal bread, to serve

Method

1 Heat the oil in a large non-stick frying pan. Add the onion and garlic, cover and cook, stirring occasionally, for 3 minutes. Add the mushrooms and cook for a further 4–5 minutes, or until the mushrooms have softened slightly. Add the courgette.

2 Beat together the eggs, egg whites and water with salt and pepper to taste.

3 Pour the egg mixture into the frying pan. Increase the heat slightly and cook, using a fork or spatula to draw the egg into the centre of the pan from the edges.

4 When the omelette is set on the base, sprinkle over the yellow pepper, the cheese, if using, and the basil. Cook for a further 3–4 minutes, or until set to your liking. Cut the omelette into wedges, garnish with rocket and serve with wholemeal bread.

CLASSIC STIR-FRIED VEGETABLES

Serves: 4 **Prep: 10 mins** **Cook: 10 mins**

Ingredients

3 tbsp sesame oil

8 spring onions, chopped

1 garlic clove, crushed

1 tbsp grated fresh ginger

1 head of broccoli, cut into florets

1 orange or yellow pepper, deseeded and roughly chopped

125 g/4½ oz red cabbage, shredded

125 g/4½ oz baby corn

175 g/6 oz portobello mushrooms, thinly sliced

200 g/7 oz fresh beansprouts

250 g/9 oz canned water chestnuts, drained

4 tsp light soy sauce, or to taste

Method

1 Heat a wok over a high heat, then add the oil. Stir-fry three quarters of the chopped spring onions with the garlic and ginger for 30 seconds.

2 Add the broccoli, pepper and red cabbage and stir-fry for 1–2 minutes. Mix in the baby corn and mushrooms and stir-fry for a further 1–2 minutes.

3 Finally, add the beansprouts and water chestnuts and cook for 2 minutes. Pour in the soy sauce and stir well.

4 Serve immediately, garnished with the remaining spring onions.

FALAFEL BURGERS

Serves: 4 **Prep: 15 mins** **Cook: 5 mins**

Ingredients

800 g/1 lb 12 oz canned chickpeas, drained and rinsed

1 small onion, chopped

juice and grated rind of 1 lime

2 tsp ground coriander

2 tsp ground cumin

6 tbsp plain flour

4 tbsp olive oil

watercress, to garnish

ready-made tomato salsa, to serve

Method

1 Put the chickpeas, onion, lime juice and rind and the spices into a food processor and process to a coarse paste.

2 Tip out onto a clean work surface and shape into 4 patties.

3 Spread out the flour on a large flat plate and turn the patties in it to coat.

4 Heat the oil in a large frying pan, add the patties and cook for 2 minutes on each side, until crisp. Garnish with watercress and serve immediately with the salsa.

KALE STIR-FRY

Serves: 4 **Prep: 20–25 mins** **Cook: 15 mins**

Ingredients

750 g/1 lb 10 oz kale

2 tbsp sunflower oil

1 onion, chopped

4 large garlic cloves, finely chopped

2 red peppers, deseeded and thinly sliced

1 large carrot, coarsely grated

100 g/3½ oz broccoli, cut into very small florets

pinch of dried chilli flakes (optional)

125 ml/4 fl oz vegetable stock

115 g/4 oz mixed sprouted beans

handful of toasted cashew nuts, chopped

salt and pepper

lemon wedges, to serve

Method

1 Using a sharp knife, cut out the thick central stems from the kale. Stack several leaves on top of each other, then cut across them to finely shred; repeat until all the kale is shredded. Set aside.

2 Heat a large wok with a lid over a high heat until a splash of water 'dances' on the surface. Add the oil and swirl it around. Add the onion and stir-fry for about 3 minutes, then add the garlic, peppers and carrot and continue stir-frying until the onion is tender and the peppers are starting to soften.

3 Add the broccoli and chilli flakes, if using, and stir. Add the kale to the wok and stir. Add the stock and salt and pepper to taste, reduce the heat to medium, cover the wok and simmer for about 5 minutes, until the kale is tender.

4 Remove the lid and allow any excess liquid to evaporate. Use 2 forks to mix the sprouted beans through the other ingredients, then adjust the seasoning, adding salt and pepper if needed.

5 Transfer to serving plates, scatter over the nuts and serve with lemon wedges.

TOFU PARCELS

Serves: 4   **Prep: 15 mins**   **Cook: 10–15 mins**

Ingredients

2 tbsp olive oil, plus extra for brushing

1 garlic clove, crushed

250 g/9 oz firm tofu, cut into chunks

250 g/9 oz cherry tomatoes, halved

1 small red onion, thinly sliced

handful of fresh basil leaves

salt and pepper

crusty bread, to serve

Method

1 Preheat the oven to 220°C/425°F/Gas Mark 7. Brush four 30-cm/12-inch squares of double-thickness foil with the oil. Mix the remaining oil with the garlic.

2 Divide the tofu, tomatoes, onion and basil between the foil squares, sprinkle with salt and pepper to taste and spoon over the garlic-flavoured oil.

3 Fold over the foil to enclose the filling and seal firmly. Place on a baking sheet in the preheated oven and cook for 10–15 minutes until heated through.

4 Carefully open the parcels and serve with crusty bread to mop up the juices.

QUICK & EASY

CHILLI BROCCOLI PASTA

Serves: 4   **Prep: 15 mins**   **Cook: 25 mins**

Ingredients

225 g/8 oz dried tortiglioni

225 g/8 oz broccoli

50 ml/2 fl oz extra virgin olive oil

2 large garlic cloves, chopped

2 fresh red chillies, deseeded and diced

8 cherry tomatoes, halved if large (optional)

salt

small handful of chopped fresh basil or parsley, to garnish

Method

1 Bring a large saucepan of lightly salted water to the boil. Add the pasta, return to the boil and cook for 8–10 minutes, until the pasta is tender but still firm to the bite. Remove from the heat, drain, rinse with cold water and drain again. Set aside.

2 Meanwhile, cut the broccoli into florets. Bring a saucepan of lightly salted water to the boil, add the broccoli and cook for 5 minutes. Drain, rinse with cold water and drain again.

3 Heat the oil in the pan that the pasta was cooked in. Add the garlic, chillies and tomatoes, if using. Cook over a high heat for 1 minute.

4 Return the broccoli to the pan and mix well. Cook for 2 minutes to heat through. Add the pasta and mix well again. Cook for a further minute.

5 Remove the pasta from the heat, tip into a large serving bowl and serve, garnished with basil.

CAULIFLOWER CHEESE

Serves: 4–6   **Prep: 20 mins**   **Cook: 20 mins**

Ingredients

1 cauliflower, trimmed and cut into florets (675 g/1 lb 8 oz prepared weight)

40 g/1½ oz butter

40 g/1½ oz plain flour

450 ml/16 fl oz milk

115 g/4 oz vegetarian Cheddar cheese, finely grated

whole nutmeg, for grating

1 tbsp freshly grated vegetarian Parmesan-style cheese

salt and pepper

Method

1 Bring a saucepan of lightly salted water to the boil, add the cauliflower, bring back to the boil and cook for 4–5 minutes. It should still be firm. Drain, place in a warmed 1.4-litre/2½-pint gratin dish and keep warm.

2 Melt the butter in the rinsed-out pan over a medium heat and stir in the flour. Cook for 1 minute, stirring constantly.

3 Remove the pan from the heat and gradually stir in the milk until you have a smooth consistency.

4 Return the pan to a low heat and continue to stir while the sauce comes to the boil and thickens. Reduce the heat and simmer gently, stirring constantly, for about 3 minutes, until the sauce is creamy and smooth.

5 Remove from the heat and stir in the Cheddar cheese and a good grating of the nutmeg. Taste and season well with salt and pepper. Meanwhile, preheat the grill to high.

6 Pour the hot sauce over the cauliflower, top with the Parmesan-style cheese and place under the preheated grill to brown. Serve immediately.

BROCCOLI WITH PEANUTS

Serves: 4 **Prep: 15 mins** **Cook: 8–10 mins**

Ingredients

3 tbsp vegetable or groundnut oil

1 lemon grass stem, roughly chopped

2 fresh red chillies, deseeded and chopped

2.5-cm/1-inch piece fresh ginger, grated

3 kaffir lime leaves, roughly torn

3 tbsp Thai green curry paste

1 onion, chopped

1 red pepper, deseeded and chopped

350 g/12 oz broccoli, cut into florets

115 g/4 oz French beans

55 g/2 oz unsalted peanuts

Method

1 Put 2 tablespoons of the oil, the lemon grass, chillies, ginger, lime leaves and curry paste into a food processor or blender and process to a paste.

2 Heat a wok over a medium heat and add the remaining oil. Add the spice paste, onion and red pepper and stir-fry for 2–3 minutes, until the vegetables start to soften. Add the broccoli and French beans, cover and cook over a low heat, stirring occasionally, for 4–5 minutes, until tender.

3 Meanwhile, toast or dry-fry the peanuts until lightly browned. Add them to the broccoli mixture and toss together. Serve immediately.

EGGS WITH FRIED TOMATO, ONION & PEPPERS

Serves: 4   **Prep: 10 mins**   **Cook: 30 mins**

Ingredients

4 large ripe tomatoes

1½ tbsp rapeseed oil

1 large onion, finely chopped

½ tsp coriander seeds, crushed

½ tsp caraway seeds, crushed

2 red peppers, deseeded and diced

¼ tsp dried chilli flakes

1 large garlic clove, thinly sliced

4 eggs

sea salt and pepper

chopped fresh flat-leaf parsley, to garnish

Method

1 Put the tomatoes into a shallow bowl and cover with boiling water. Leave for 30 seconds, then drain.

2 Slip off the tomato skins and discard. Chop the flesh, reserving the seeds and juice.

3 Heat the oil in a large, non-stick frying pan over a medium heat. Add the onion, coriander seeds and caraway seeds. Fry, stirring occasionally, for about 10 minutes, until the onion is soft and golden.

4 Stir in the red peppers and chilli flakes. Fry for about 5 minutes, until soft.

5 Add the garlic and tomatoes with their seeds and juices and season with salt and pepper. Simmer, uncovered, over a low heat for 10 minutes.

6 Crack the eggs over the surface. Cover and cook for a further 3–4 minutes, or until the eggs are set. Season with salt and pepper to taste, sprinkle with parsley and serve immediately.

QUICK & EASY

SPAGHETTI OLIO E AGLIO

Serves: 4   **Prep: 10 mins**   **Cook: 15 mins**

Ingredients

450 g/1 lb dried spaghetti

125 ml/4 fl oz extra virgin olive oil

3 garlic cloves, finely chopped

3 tbsp chopped fresh flat-leaf parsley

salt and pepper

Method

1 Bring a large saucepan of lightly salted water to the boil. Add the pasta, bring back to the boil and cook for 8–10 minutes, until tender but still firm to the bite.

2 Meanwhile, heat the oil in a heavy-based frying pan. Add the garlic and a pinch of salt and cook over a low heat, stirring constantly, for 3–4 minutes, or until golden. Do not allow the garlic to brown or it will taste bitter. Remove the frying pan from the heat.

3 Drain the pasta and transfer to a warmed serving dish. Pour in the garlic-flavoured oil, then add the chopped parsley and season to taste with salt and pepper. Toss well and serve immediately.

★ Variation

Add a pinch of chilli flakes to the pan with the garlic for a spicy version of this classic dish.

QUICK & EASY

FAMILY FAVOURITES

VEGETARIAN CHILLI BURGERS 108

CARROT & CORIANDER SAUSAGES & MASH 110

SPICY VEGETABLE LASAGNE 112

SPRING STEW 114

VEGETARIAN HOT DOGS 116

SWEET POTATO CURRY WITH LENTILS 118

VEGETABLE PIE 119

SWEET POTATO & HALLOUMI BURGERS 120

VEGETABLE CHILLI 122

LENTIL BOLOGNESE 124

CHILLI TOFU TORTILLAS 126

SOUFFLÉ JACKET POTATOES 128

MACARONI CHEESE 129

LAYERED POTATO & MUSHROOM PIE 130

HOPPIN' JOHN 131

SWEET POTATO RAVIOLI WITH SAGE BUTTER 132

COURGETTE, PEPPER & TOMATO GRATIN 134

THAI TOFU CAKES WITH CHILLI DIP 136

RATATOUILLE & POTATO WEDGES 138

BAKED AUBERGINE WITH TOMATO SAUCE 140

SPINACH & RICOTTA CANNELLONI 142

GRIDDLED COURGETTE & FETA PIZZA 144

NEW POTATO, FETA & HERB FRITTATA 146

PARSNIP LAYERED CASSEROLE 147

RIGATONI WITH ROAST COURGETTE & TOMATO SAUCE .. 148

ROAST BUTTERNUT SQUASH 150

PENNE IN TOMATO SAUCE WITH TWO CHEESES 152

BEAN & TOMATO CASSEROLE WITH PARMESAN TOASTS .. 154

VEGETARIAN CHILLI BURGERS

Serves: 4–6

Prep: 35 mins,
plus chilling

Cook: 25–30 mins

Ingredients

85 g/3 oz bulgar wheat

300 g/10½ oz canned red kidney beans, drained and rinsed

300 g/10½ oz canned cannellini beans, drained and rinsed

1–2 fresh red jalapeño chillies, deseeded and roughly chopped

2–3 garlic cloves

6 spring onions, roughly chopped

1 yellow pepper, deseeded, peeled and chopped

1 tbsp chopped fresh coriander

115 g/4 oz mature vegetarian Cheddar cheese, grated

2 tbsp wholemeal flour

1–2 tbsp sunflower oil

1 large tomato, sliced

salt and pepper

wholemeal buns, to serve

Method

1 Place the bulgar wheat in a sieve and rinse under cold running water. Cook the bulgar wheat in a saucepan of lightly salted water for 12 minutes, or until tender. Drain and reserve.

2 Place the beans in a food processor with the chillies, garlic, spring onions, yellow pepper, coriander and half the cheese. Using the pulse button, chop finely. Add to the cooked bulgar wheat with salt and pepper to taste. Mix well, then shape into four to six equal-sized burgers. Cover and leave to chill for 1 hour. Coat the burgers in the flour.

3 Preheat the grill to medium. Heat a heavy-based frying pan and add the oil. When hot, add the burgers and cook over a medium heat for 5–6 minutes on each side, or until piping hot. Place one to two slices of tomato on top of each burger and sprinkle with the remaining cheese. Cook under the hot grill for 2–3 minutes, or until the cheese begins to melt. Serve in wholemeal buns.

★ **Variation**

Pile your burger high with extra fillings like lettuce leaves, fried onions and your favourite sauce.

CARROT & CORIANDER SAUSAGES & MASH

Serves: 4

Prep: 25 mins, plus cooling & chilling

Cook: 25–30 mins

Ingredients

Sausages

1 tbsp olive oil

25 g/1 oz spring onions, chopped

1 garlic clove, chopped

½ fresh red chilli, deseeded and finely chopped

1 tsp ground cumin

450 g/1 lb carrot, grated

½ tsp salt

3 tbsp crunchy peanut butter

25 g/1 oz finely chopped fresh coriander, plus extra to garnish

100 g/3½ oz fresh brown breadcrumbs

plain flour, for dusting

vegetable oil, for frying

Mash

900 g/2 lb floury potatoes, chopped

3 tbsp milk

55 g/2 oz margarine or butter

salt and pepper

Method

1 To make the sausages, heat the olive oil in a large saucepan over a medium heat. Fry the spring onions, garlic, chilli and cumin for 2 minutes. Stir in the carrot and salt and mix well. Cover the pan and cook on a very low heat for 6–8 minutes, or until the carrot is tender.

2 Transfer the carrot mixture to a large mixing bowl and mix in the peanut butter and coriander, ensuring that the ingredients are thoroughly combined. Allow the mixture to cool, and then mix in the breadcrumbs.

3 On a floured surface, form the mixture into eight large sausages. Leave to chill in the refrigerator for up to an hour. Heat the vegetable oil in a frying pan over a medium heat and fry the sausages gently for 10 minutes, turning occasionally, until browned.

4 Meanwhile, bring a large saucepan of lightly salted water to the boil. Add the potatoes, bring back to the boil and cook for 15–20 minutes, or until cooked through and fluffy. Transfer to a mixing bowl, add the milk and margarine and mash the mixture thoroughly until all lumps are removed. Season to taste with salt and pepper.

5 Place the mashed potato on warmed plates and top with the sausages. Garnish with coriander and serve.

SPICY VEGETABLE LASAGNE

Serves: 4　　　**Prep: 25–30 mins,**　　　**Cook: 55 mins**
plus standing

Ingredients

1 aubergine, sliced

3 tbsp olive oil

2 garlic cloves, crushed

1 red onion, halved and sliced

3 mixed peppers, deseeded and diced

225 g/8 oz mushrooms, sliced

2 celery sticks, sliced

1 courgette, diced

½ tsp chilli powder

½ tsp ground cumin

2 tomatoes, chopped

300 ml/10 fl oz passata

3 tbsp chopped fresh basil

8 dried no pre-cook lasagne sheets

salt and pepper

Cheese sauce

2 tbsp butter

1 tbsp flour

150 ml/5 fl oz vegetable stock

300 ml/10 fl oz milk

75 g/2¾ oz vegetarian Cheddar cheese, grated

1 tsp Dijon mustard

1 egg, beaten

Method

1 Place the aubergine slices in a colander, sprinkle with salt and leave for 20 minutes. Rinse under cold water, drain and reserve.

2 Preheat the oven to 180°C/350°F/Gas Mark 4. Heat the oil in a saucepan. Add the garlic and onion and sauté for 1–2 minutes. Add the peppers, mushrooms, celery and courgette and cook, stirring constantly, for 3–4 minutes.

3 Stir in the chilli powder and cumin and cook for 1 minute. Mix in the tomatoes, passata and 2 tablespoons of the basil and season to taste with salt and pepper.

4 For the sauce, melt the butter in a saucepan. Stir in the flour and cook for 1 minute. Remove from the heat, gradually stir in the stock and milk, return to the heat, then add half the cheese and all the mustard. Boil, stirring, until thickened. Stir in the remaining basil. Remove from the heat and stir in the egg.

5 Place half the lasagne sheets in an ovenproof dish. Top with half the vegetable and tomato sauce, then half the aubergines. Repeat and then spoon the cheese sauce on top. Sprinkle with the remaining cheese and bake in the preheated oven for 40 minutes, until golden and bubbling. Serve immediately.

FAMILY FAVOURITES

SPRING STEW

Serves: 4   **Prep: 20 mins**   **Cook: 35 mins**

Ingredients

2 tbsp olive oil

4–8 baby onions, halved

1 celery stick, sliced

225 g/8 oz baby carrots, scrubbed, and halved if large

300 g/10½ oz new potatoes, scrubbed and halved, or quartered if large

850 ml–1.2 litres/1½–2 pints vegetable stock

400 g/14 oz canned haricot beans, drained and rinsed

1 fresh bouquet garni

1½–2 tbsp light soy sauce

85 g/3 oz baby sweetcorn

115 g/4 oz frozen or shelled fresh broad beans, thawed if frozen

½–1 Savoy or spring cabbage, about 225 g/8 oz

1½ tbsp cornflour

2 tbsp cold water

salt and pepper

freshly grated vegetarian Parmesan-style cheese, to serve

Method

1 Heat the oil in a large, heavy-based saucepan with a tight-fitting lid. Add the onions, celery, carrots and potatoes and cook, stirring frequently, for 5 minutes, or until softened. Add the stock, drained beans, bouquet garni and soy sauce, then bring to the boil. Reduce the heat, cover and simmer for 12 minutes.

2 Add the baby sweetcorn and broad beans and season to taste with salt and pepper. Simmer for a further 3 minutes.

3 Meanwhile, discard the outer leaves and hard central core from the cabbage and shred the leaves. Add to the saucepan and simmer for a further 3–5 minutes, or until all the vegetables are tender.

4 Blend the cornflour with the water, stir into the saucepan and cook, stirring, for 4–6 minutes, or until the liquid has thickened. Serve with a bowl of Parmesan cheese for stirring into the stew.

VEGETARIAN HOT DOGS

Serves: 4

Prep: 25 mins,
plus chilling

Cook: 15 mins

Ingredients

1 tbsp sunflower oil, plus extra for frying

1 small onion, finely chopped

50 g/1¾ oz mushrooms, finely chopped

½ red pepper, deseeded and finely chopped

400 g/14 oz canned cannellini beans, drained and rinsed

100 g/3½ oz fresh breadcrumbs

100 g/3½ oz vegetarian Cheddar cheese, grated

1 tsp dried mixed herbs

1 egg yolk

seasoned plain flour

To serve

small bread rolls

fried onion slices

tomato chutney

Method

1 Heat the sunflower oil in a saucepan. Add the onion, mushrooms and pepper and fry until softened.

2 Mash the cannellini beans in a large bowl. Add the onion, mushroom and pepper mixture, the breadcrumbs, cheese, herbs and egg yolk and mix well. Press the mixture together with your fingers and shape into eight sausages. Roll each sausage in the seasoned flour. Leave to chill in the refrigerator for at least 30 minutes.

3 Heat the vegetable oil in a frying pan over a medium heat and fry the sausages gently for 10 minutes, turning occasionally, until browned. Split bread rolls down the centre and insert a layer of fried onions. Place the sausages in the rolls and serve with tomato chutney.

SWEET POTATO CURRY WITH LENTILS

Serves: 4   **Prep: 15 mins**   **Cook: 35 mins**

Ingredients

1 tsp vegetable oil

100 g/3½ oz sweet potato, cut into bite-sized cubes

75 g/2¾ oz potato, cut into bite-sized cubes

1 small onion, finely chopped

1 small garlic clove, finely chopped

1 small fresh green chilli, deseeded and chopped

½ tsp ground ginger

50 g/1¾ oz green lentils

75–100 ml/2½–3½ fl oz hot vegetable stock

½ tsp garam masala

1 tbsp natural yogurt

pepper

Method

1 Heat the oil in a saucepan with a lid and sauté the sweet potato over a medium heat, turning occasionally, for 5 minutes.

2 Meanwhile, cook the potato in a saucepan of boiling water for 6 minutes, until almost cooked. Drain and set aside.

3 Remove the sweet potato from the pan with a slotted spoon, then add the onion to the pan. Cook, stirring occasionally, for 5 minutes, or until transparent. Add the garlic, chilli and ginger and stir for 1 minute.

4 Return the sweet potato to the pan with the boiled potato and the lentils, half the stock, the garam masala and pepper to taste. Stir well to combine, bring to a simmer and cover.

5 Reduce the heat and simmer for 20 minutes, adding the rest of the stock if the curry looks too dry. Stir in the yogurt and serve immediately.

VEGETABLE PIE

Serves: 4   **Prep: 20 mins, plus cooling**   **Cook: 40 mins**

Ingredients

175 g/6 oz carrots, chopped

140 g/5 oz broccoli florets

115 g/4 oz broad beans, shelled weight, fresh or frozen

55 g/2 oz sweetcorn kernels, canned or frozen

300 ml/10 fl oz vegetable stock

1 tbsp cornflour

2 tbsp water

1 tbsp chopped fresh coriander

3 sheets filo pastry

pepper

Method

1 Preheat the oven to 190°C/375°F/Gas Mark 5. Cook the carrots in a saucepan of boiling water for 6 minutes, then add the broccoli florets with the broad beans and cook for a further 2 minutes. Stir in the sweetcorn, mix then drain thoroughly and reserve.

2 Heat the stock in another saucepan, add the vegetables and bring to boiling point. Blend the cornflour with the water in a bowl and stir the paste into the boiling liquid. Cook, stirring constantly, until the sauce thickens. Stir in the chopped coriander and add pepper to taste. Spoon the mixture into a 1.2-litre/2-pint pie dish and leave to cool.

3 Place the filo pastry on a clean work surface and brush one sheet lightly with a little water. Put a second sheet on top. Place the filo pastry over the filling, pressing the edges over the dish to encase completely.

4 Brush the top of the pie with a little water and put the remaining sheet of pastry decoratively on top. Bake in the preheated oven for 25 minutes, or until the top is golden brown. Serve immediately.

FAMILY FAVOURITES

SWEET POTATO & HALLOUMI BURGERS

Makes: 4-6

Prep: 20 mins,
plus chilling

Cook: 40-50 mins

Ingredients

450 g/1 lb sweet potatoes,
cut into chunks

175 g/6 oz broccoli florets

2–3 garlic cloves, crushed

1 red onion, finely chopped
or grated

1½–2 fresh red jalapeño
chillies, deseeded and
finely chopped

175 g/6 oz vegetarian
halloumi cheese, grated

2 tbsp wholemeal flour

2–3 tbsp sunflower oil

450 g/1 lb onions, sliced

1 tbsp chopped
fresh coriander

salt and pepper

Method

1 Cook the sweet potato in a saucepan of lightly salted boiling water for 15–20 minutes, or until tender. Drain and mash. Cut the broccoli into small pieces, cook in a separate saucepan of boiling water for 3 minutes, then drain and plunge into cold water. Drain again, then add to the mashed sweet potato.

2 Stir in the garlic, onion, chilli, cheese and salt and pepper to taste. Mix well and shape into four to six equal-sized patties, then coat in the flour. Cover and leave to chill in the refrigerator for at least 1 hour.

3 Heat 1½ tablespoons of the oil in a heavy-based frying pan. Add the onions and fry over a medium heat for 12–15 minutes, or until softened. Stir in the coriander and reserve.

4 Place the burgers in the frying pan, adding more oil if necessary. Cook over a medium heat for 5–6 minutes on each side, or until cooked through.

5 Top the burgers with the reserved fried onions and coriander and serve immediately.

VEGETABLE CHILLI

Serves: 4   **Prep: 25 mins**   **Cook: 1 hour 30 mins**

Ingredients

1 aubergine, peeled if
wished, cut into 2.5-cm/
1-inch slices

1 tbsp olive oil, plus extra
for brushing

1 large red or yellow onion,
finely chopped

2 red or yellow peppers,
deseeded and finely
chopped

3–4 garlic cloves, finely
chopped or crushed

800 g/1 lb 12 oz canned
chopped tomatoes

1 tbsp mild chilli powder,
or to taste

½ tsp ground cumin

½ tsp dried oregano

2 small courgettes,
quartered lengthways
and sliced

400 g/14 oz canned kidney
beans, drained and rinsed

450 ml/16 fl oz water

1 tbsp tomato purée

salt and pepper

chopped spring onions
and grated vegetarian
Cheddar cheese, to serve

Method

1 Brush the aubergine slices on one side with
oil. Heat half the oil in a large heavy-based
frying pan over a medium–high heat. Add the
aubergine slices, oiled-side up, and cook for
5–6 minutes, until browned on one side. Turn the
slices over, cook on the other side until browned
and transfer to a plate. Cut into bite-sized pieces.

2 Heat the remaining oil in a large saucepan over
a medium heat. Add the onion and peppers
and cook, stirring occasionally, for 3–4 minutes,
until the onion is just softened but not browned.
Add the garlic and continue cooking for
2–3 minutes, or until the onion is just beginning
to colour.

3 Add the tomatoes, chilli powder, cumin and
oregano. Season to taste with salt and pepper.
Bring just to the boil, reduce the heat, cover and
simmer gently for 15 minutes.

4 Add the courgettes, aubergine and beans.
Stir in the water and the tomato purée. Bring
back to the boil, then cover the pan and
continue simmering for about 45 minutes,
or until the vegetables are tender. Taste and
then adjust the seasoning, adding salt and
pepper if needed. Ladle into warmed bowls and
top with spring onions and cheese.

LENTIL BOLOGNESE

Serves: 4   **Prep: 15–20 mins**   **Cook: 30–40 mins**

Ingredients

175 g/6 oz green lentils

2 tbsp olive oil

1 large onion, chopped

2 garlic cloves, crushed

2 carrots, chopped

2 celery sticks, chopped

800 g/1 lb 12 oz canned chopped tomatoes

150 ml/5 fl oz vegetable stock

1 red pepper, deseeded and chopped

2 tbsp tomato purée

2 tsp very finely chopped fresh rosemary

1 tsp dried oregano

280 g/10 oz dried spaghetti or linguine

handful of basil leaves, torn

salt and pepper

freshly grated vegetarian Parmesan-style cheese, to serve

Method

1 Put the lentils in a saucepan and cover with cold water. Bring to the boil and simmer for 20–30 minutes until just tender. Drain well.

2 Meanwhile, heat the oil in a large saucepan. Add the onion, garlic, carrots and celery. Cover and cook over a low heat for 5 minutes. Stir in the tomatoes, stock, red pepper, tomato purée, rosemary and oregano. Cover and simmer for 20 minutes until the sauce is thickened and the vegetables are tender. Add the lentils and cook, stirring, for a further 5 minutes. Season with salt and pepper.

3 While the sauce is cooking, bring a large saucepan of lightly salted water to the boil. Add the spaghetti, bring back to the boil and cook for 10 minutes, or until tender but still firm to the bite. Drain well, then divide the spaghetti between four warmed bowls. Spoon the sauce over the top and scatter with the basil leaves. Serve immediately with the grated cheese on the side.

CHILLI TOFU TORTILLAS

Serves: 4   **Prep: 35 mins**   **Cook: 31–33 mins**

Ingredients

½ tsp chilli powder

1 tsp paprika

2 tbsp plain flour

225 g/8 oz firm tofu, cut into 1-cm/½-inch pieces

2 tbsp vegetable oil

1 onion, finely chopped

1 garlic clove, crushed

1 large red pepper, deseeded and finely chopped

1 large ripe avocado

1 tbsp lime juice

4 tomatoes, peeled, deseeded and chopped

125 g/4½ oz vegetarian Cheddar cheese, grated

8 soft flour tortillas

150 ml/5 fl oz soured cream

salt and pepper

pickled green jalapeño chillies, to serve

Sauce

850 ml/1½ pints passata

3 tbsp chopped fresh parsley

3 tbsp chopped fresh coriander

Method

1 Preheat the oven to 190°C/375°F/Gas Mark 5. Mix the chilli powder, paprika, flour and salt and pepper to taste on a plate and use to coat the tofu pieces.

2 Heat the oil in a frying pan and gently fry the tofu for 3–4 minutes, until golden. Remove with a slotted spoon, drain on kitchen paper and set aside.

3 Add the onion, garlic and red pepper to the oil and fry for 2–3 minutes, until just soft. Drain and set aside.

4 Halve the avocado, peel and remove the stone. Slice lengthways, put in a bowl with the lime juice and toss to coat.

5 Add the tofu and the onion mixture and gently stir in the tomatoes and half the cheese. Spoon a little of the filling down the centre of each tortilla, top with a little soured cream and roll up. Arrange the tortillas in a shallow ovenproof dish in a single layer.

6 To make the sauce, mix all the ingredients together. Spoon the sauce over the tortillas, sprinkle with the remaining cheese and bake in the preheated oven for 25 minutes, until the cheese is golden brown and bubbling. Serve the tortillas immediately with the pickled jalapeño chillies.

SOUFFLÉ JACKET POTATOES

Serves: 4　　　**Prep: 20 mins**　　　**Cook: 1 hour 17 mins–1 hour 38 mins**

Ingredients

4 large baking potatoes, about 400 g/14 oz each

oil, for brushing

2 tbsp milk or single cream

2 eggs, separated

100 g/3½ oz vegetarian Cheddar cheese, grated

15 g/½ oz butter

4 spring onions, finely chopped

salt and pepper

Method

1 Preheat the oven to 200°C/400°F/Gas Mark 6. Place the potatoes on a baking sheet, brush with oil and rub with salt. Bake in the preheated oven for 1–1¼ hours until tender. (Do not turn off the oven.)

2 Cut a slice from the top of the potatoes and scoop out the flesh, leaving about a 5-mm/¼-inch thick shell. Put the flesh into a bowl. Add the milk, egg yolks and half the cheese and mash together.

3 Melt the butter in a small saucepan, add the spring onions and stir-fry for 1–2 minutes until soft. Reserve a spoonful for the garnish. Stir into the potato mixture and season to taste with salt and pepper.

4 Whisk the egg whites in a grease-free bowl until they hold soft peaks. Fold them lightly into the potato mixture, then spoon the mixture back into the shells.

5 Place the filled potatoes on the baking sheet and sprinkle the remaining cheese on top. Bake for 15–20 minutes until golden. Garnish with the reserved spring onions and serve immediately.

FAMILY FAVOURITES

MACARONI CHEESE

Serves: 4   **Prep: 15–20 mins**   **Cook: 30–35 mins**

Ingredients

250 g/9 oz dried macaroni pasta

600 ml/1 pint milk

½ tsp grated nutmeg

55 g/2 oz butter, plus extra for cooking the pasta

55 g/2 oz plain flour

200 g/7 oz mature vegetarian Cheddar cheese, grated

55 g/2 oz freshly grated vegetarian Parmesan-style cheese

200 g/7 oz baby spinach

salt and pepper

Method

1 Cook the macaroni according to the instructions on the packet. Remove from the heat, drain and add a small knob of butter to keep it soft. Return to the saucepan and cover to keep warm.

2 Put the milk and nutmeg into a saucepan over a low heat and heat until warm, but do not boil. Put the butter into a heavy-based saucepan over a low heat, melt the butter, add the flour and stir to make a roux. Cook gently for 2 minutes. Add the milk a little at a time, whisking it into the roux, then cook for about 10–15 minutes to make a loose, custard-style sauce.

3 Add three quarters of the Cheddar cheese and the Parmesan-style cheese and stir through until they have melted in, then add the spinach, season to taste with salt and pepper and remove from the heat.

4 Preheat the grill to high. Put the macaroni into a shallow heatproof dish, then pour the sauce over. Scatter the remaining cheese over the top and place the dish under the preheated grill. Grill until the cheese begins to brown, then serve immediately.

FAMILY FAVOURITES

LAYERED POTATO & MUSHROOM PIE

Serves: 2–4   **Prep: 20 mins**   **Cook: 55 mins**

Ingredients

butter, for greasing

500 g/1 lb 2 oz waxy potatoes, thinly sliced and parboiled

150 g/5½ oz mixed mushrooms, sliced

1 tbsp chopped fresh rosemary

4 tbsp snipped chives, plus extra to garnish

2 garlic cloves, crushed

150 ml/5 fl oz double cream

salt and pepper

Method

1. Preheat the oven to 190°C/375°F/Gas Mark 5. Grease a large baking dish with butter.

2. Layer a quarter of the potatoes in the base of the dish. Arrange one third of the mushrooms on top of the potatoes and sprinkle with one third of the rosemary, chives and garlic. Continue making the layers in the same order, and finish with a layer of potatoes on top.

3. Pour the double cream evenly over the top of the potatoes. Season to taste.

4. Bake in the preheated oven for 45 minutes, until golden brown. Garnish with snipped chives and serve immediately.

FAMILY FAVOURITES

HOPPIN' JOHN

Serves: 6

Prep: 10–15 mins,
plus overnight soaking

Cook: 2 hours 25 mins–
2 hours 30 mins

Ingredients

225 g/8 oz dried black-eyed
beans, soaked overnight
and drained

225 g/8 oz long-grain rice

Tomato sauce

25 g/1 oz butter

2 tbsp corn oil

1 onion, finely chopped

400 g/14 oz canned
chopped tomatoes

2 tbsp tomato purée

brown sugar, to taste

½ tsp cayenne pepper

100 ml/3½ fl oz water

salt and pepper

Method

1 Put the beans into a large saucepan and pour in water to cover. Bring to the boil and boil vigorously for 15 minutes, then remove from the heat and drain. Return the beans to the pan and pour in the 1.2 litres/2 pints of water. Bring to the boil, then reduce the heat, partially cover the pan and simmer for 1½ hours.

2 Meanwhile, make the sauce. Melt the butter with the oil in a saucepan. Add the onion and cook over a low heat, stirring occasionally, for 5 minutes, until softened. Stir in the tomatoes, tomato purée, sugar to taste, cayenne and water and season to taste with salt and pepper. Increase the heat to medium and bring to the boil, then reduce the heat and simmer, stirring occasionally, for 15 minutes, until thickened.

3 Stir the rice into the pan of beans, cover and simmer for a further 15 minutes.

4 Stir the sauce into the bean and rice mixture, re-cover the pan and simmer for a further 15–20 minutes, until the rice and beans are tender. Serve immediately.

FAMILY FAVOURITES

SWEET POTATO RAVIOLI WITH SAGE BUTTER

Serves: 4

Prep: 45 mins, plus chilling

Cook: 35 mins

Ingredients

400 g/14 oz type 00 pasta flour

4 eggs, beaten

semolina, for dusting

salt

Filling

500 g/1 lb 2 oz sweet potatoes

3 tbsp olive oil

1 large onion, finely chopped

1 garlic clove, crushed

1 tsp chopped fresh thyme

2 tbsp runny honey

salt and pepper

Sage butter

50 g/1¾ oz butter

1 bunch of fresh sage leaves, finely chopped, plus extra leaves to garnish

Method

1 To make the pasta dough, sift the flour into a large bowl or food processor. Add the eggs and bring the mixture together or process to make a soft but not sticky dough. Turn out onto a work surface lightly dusted with semolina and knead for 4–5 minutes, until smooth. Cover with clingfilm and chill in the refrigerator for at least 30 minutes.

2 For the filling, peel the sweet potatoes and cut into chunks. Cook in a saucepan of boiling water for 20 minutes, or until tender. Drain and mash.

3 Heat the oil in a frying pan over a medium heat, add the onion and cook, stirring frequently, for 4–5 minutes, until softened but not coloured. Stir the onion into the mashed potatoes and add the garlic and thyme. Drizzle with the honey and season to taste with salt and pepper. Set aside.

4 Using a pasta machine, roll the pasta out to a thickness of about 1 mm/¹⁄₃₂ inch (or use a rolling pin on a work surface lightly dusted with semolina).

5 Cut the pasta in half. Place teaspoonfuls of the filling at evenly spaced intervals across half of the pasta. Brush around the filling with a small amount of water and cover with the second half

of the pasta. Press lightly around the filling to seal and cut into squares with a sharp knife or pastry wheel. Lay the ravioli out on a sheet of greaseproof paper that has been lightly dusted with semolina.

6 Bring a large saucepan of salted water to the boil and drop in the ravioli. Cook for 2–3 minutes, until the pasta rises to the surface and is tender but still firm to the bite.

7 Meanwhile, for the sage butter, melt the butter with the chopped sage in a small saucepan over a low heat.

8 Drain the ravioli and immediately toss with the sage butter. Serve immediately, garnished with sage leaves.

COURGETTE, PEPPER & TOMATO GRATIN

Serves: 4   **Prep: 20 mins**   **Cook: 45 mins**

Ingredients

25 g/1 oz butter

2 tbsp olive oil

1 onion, thinly sliced

2 garlic cloves, finely chopped

1 celery stick, finely chopped

700 g/1 lb 9 oz courgettes, sliced

2 large red peppers, deseeded and sliced

55 g/2 oz button mushrooms, sliced

400 g/14 oz canned chopped tomatoes

2 tbsp tomato purée

brown sugar, to taste

1 tbsp chopped fresh basil

1 bay leaf

100 ml/3½ fl oz water

55 g/2 oz vegetarian Parmesan-style cheese, grated

salt and pepper

Method

1 Melt the butter with the oil in a large saucepan. Add the onion, garlic, celery, courgettes, peppers and mushrooms and cook over a low heat, stirring occasionally, for 5 minutes, until softened. Stir in the tomatoes, tomato purée, sugar to taste, basil, bay leaf and water and season to taste with salt and pepper. Increase the heat to medium and bring to the boil, then reduce the heat and simmer, stirring occasionally, for 30 minutes, until thickened and the vegetables are tender.

2 Meanwhile, preheat the grill. Remove and discard the bay leaf and spoon the vegetable mixture into a flameproof dish. Sprinkle with the cheese and cook under the preheated grill for 3–5 minutes, until the top is golden brown and bubbling. Serve immediately.

THAI TOFU CAKES WITH CHILLI DIP

Serves: 4

Prep: 25–30 mins, plus chilling

Cook: 10–15 mins

Ingredients

300 g/10½ oz firm tofu, drained weight, coarsely grated

1 lemon grass stalk, finely chopped

2 garlic cloves, chopped

2.5-cm/1-inch piece fresh ginger, grated

2 kaffir lime leaves, finely chopped (optional)

2 shallots, finely chopped

2 fresh red chillies, deseeded and finely chopped

4 tbsp chopped fresh coriander

90 g/3¼ oz plain flour, plus extra for dusting

½ tsp salt

corn oil, for cooking

Chilli dip

3 tbsp white distilled vinegar

2 spring onions, finely sliced

1 tbsp caster sugar

2 fresh chillies, chopped

2 tbsp chopped fresh coriander

pinch of salt

Method

1 To make the chilli dip, mix all the ingredients together in a small serving bowl and set aside.

2 Mix the tofu with the lemon grass, garlic, ginger, lime leaves, if using, shallots, chillies and coriander in a mixing bowl. Stir in the flour and salt to make a coarse, sticky paste. Cover and chill in the refrigerator for 1 hour to let the mixture firm up slightly.

3 Form the mixture into eight large walnut-sized balls and, using floured hands, flatten into circles. Heat enough oil to cover the bottom of a large, heavy-based frying pan over medium heat. Cook the cakes in two batches, turning halfway through, for 4–6 minutes, or until golden brown and cooked through. Drain on kitchen paper and serve warm with the chilli dip.

RATATOUILLE & POTATO WEDGES

Serves: 4 **Prep: 25 mins** **Cook: 55–60 mins**

Ingredients

300 g/10½ oz potatoes

200 g/7 oz aubergine, cut into wedges

125 g/4½ oz red onion, cut into rings

200 g/7 oz mixed peppers, deseeded and sliced

175 g/6 oz courgettes, sliced

125 g/4½ oz cherry tomatoes

90 g/3¼ oz fat-free fromage frais

1 tsp runny honey

pinch of smoked paprika

1 tsp chopped fresh flat-leaf parsley, to garnish

Marinade

1 tsp vegetable oil

1 tbsp lemon juice

4 tbsp vegetarian white wine

1 tsp sugar

2 tbsp chopped fresh basil

1 tsp chopped fresh rosemary

1 tbsp chopped lemon thyme

¼ tsp smoked paprika

Method

1 Preheat the oven to 200°C/400°F/Gas Mark 6.

2 Bake the potatoes in their skins in the oven for 30 minutes. Remove and cut into wedges – the flesh should not be completely cooked.

3 To make the marinade, put all the ingredients in a bowl and blend together with a hand-held electric blender until smooth, or use a food processor.

4 Put the potato wedges into a large bowl with the aubergine, onion, peppers and courgettes, pour over the marinade and mix thoroughly.

5 Arrange the vegetables on a non-stick baking sheet and roast in the preheated oven, turning occasionally, for 25–30 minutes, or until golden brown and tender. Add the tomatoes for the last 5 minutes of the cooking time just to split the skins and warm slightly.

6 Mix the fromage frais, honey and paprika together in a bowl.

7 Garnish the vegetables with parsley and serve with a little fromage frais mixture.

BAKED AUBERGINE WITH TOMATO SAUCE

Serves: 6 **Prep: 25–30 mins** **Cook: 55–60 mins**

Ingredients

40 g/1½ oz butter, plus extra for greasing

40 g/1½ oz dry breadcrumbs

1 large aubergine, cut into 1-cm/½-inch slices

1 tsp dried oregano

55 g/2 oz vegetarian Parmesan-style cheese, grated

salt

Tomato sauce

25 g/1 oz butter

2 tbsp olive oil

1 small onion, finely chopped

1 garlic clove, finely chopped

1 celery stick, finely chopped

400 g/14 oz canned chopped tomatoes

2 tbsp tomato purée

brown sugar, to taste

1 tbsp chopped fresh basil, plus extra to garnish

1 tsp dried oregano

100 ml/3½ fl oz water

salt and pepper

Method

1 First, make the sauce. Melt the butter with the oil in a saucepan. Add the onion, garlic and celery and cook over a low heat, stirring occasionally, for 5 minutes, until softened. Stir in the tomatoes, tomato purée, sugar to taste, basil, oregano and water and season to taste with salt and pepper. Increase the heat to medium and bring to the boil, then reduce the heat and simmer, stirring occasionally, for 15–20 minutes, until thickened.

2 Preheat the oven to 230°C/450°F/Gas Mark 8. Grease a baking sheet with butter. Melt the butter and pour it into a shallow dish. Spread out the breadcrumbs in a separate shallow dish. Dip the aubergine slices first in the melted butter and then in the breadcrumbs to coat. Put them on the prepared baking sheet and season to taste with salt. Bake in the preheated oven for 20 minutes, until golden brown and tender.

3 Remove the baking sheet from the oven. Top each aubergine slice with a spoonful of tomato sauce and sprinkle with a little of the oregano and cheese. Return to the oven and bake for a further 10 minutes, until the topping is golden brown. Transfer to a serving dish, garnish with basil and serve immediately.

SPINACH & RICOTTA CANNELLONI

Serves: 4 **Prep: 25 mins** **Cook: 50–55 mins**

Ingredients

melted butter, for greasing

12 dried cannelloni tubes, each about 7.5 cm/ 3 inches long

salt and pepper

Filling

140 g/5 oz frozen spinach, thawed and drained

115 g/4 oz vegetarian ricotta cheese

1 egg

3 tbsp grated vegetarian pecorino-style cheese

pinch of freshly grated nutmeg

Cheese sauce

25 g/1 oz butter

2 tbsp plain flour

600 ml/1 pint hot milk

85 g/3 oz vegetarian Gruyère cheese, grated

Method

1 Preheat the oven to 180°C/350°F/Gas Mark 4. Grease a rectangular ovenproof dish with the melted butter.

2 Bring a large saucepan of lightly salted water to the boil. Add the pasta, bring back to the boil and cook for 6–7 minutes, until nearly tender. Drain and rinse, then spread out on a clean tea towel.

3 For the filling, put the spinach and ricotta into a food processor or blender and process briefly until combined. Add the egg and pecorino-style cheese and process to a smooth paste. Transfer to a bowl, add the nutmeg and season to taste with salt and pepper.

4 Spoon the filling into a piping bag fitted with a 1-cm/½-inch nozzle. Carefully open a cannelloni tube and pipe in a little of the filling. Place the filled tube in the prepared dish and repeat.

5 For the cheese sauce, melt the butter in a saucepan. Add the flour to the butter and cook over a low heat, stirring constantly, for 1 minute. Remove from the heat and gradually stir in the hot milk. Return to the heat and bring to the boil,

stirring constantly. Simmer over a low heat, stirring frequently, for 10 minutes, until thickened and smooth.

6 Remove from the heat, stir in the Gruyère cheese and season to taste with salt and pepper.

7 Spoon the cheese sauce over the filled cannelloni. Cover the dish with foil and bake in the preheated oven for 20–25 minutes. Serve immediately.

GRIDDLED COURGETTE & FETA PIZZA

Makes: 2 pizzas

Prep: 35 mins, plus rising

Cook: 15–20 mins

Ingredients

Basic pizza dough

300 g/10½ oz strong white flour, plus extra for dusting

1 tsp easy-blend dried yeast

1½ tsp salt

175 ml/6 fl oz hand-hot water

1 tbsp olive oil, plus extra for kneading

Topping

1 tbsp olive oil

1 garlic clove, crushed

1 large courgette, sliced lengthways

200 g/7 oz passata

250 g/9 oz vegetarian feta cheese, drained and crumbled

salt and pepper

fresh mint leaves, roughly torn, to garnish

Method

1 Sift the flour into a mixing bowl and add the yeast and salt, making a small well in the top. Mix the water and oil together and pour into the bowl, using a round-bladed knife to gradually combine all the flour to make a sticky dough.

2 Lightly flour the work surface and your hands and knead the dough for about 10 minutes, until it is smooth and elastic.

3 Cover the dough with some lightly oiled clingfilm or a damp tea towel and leave to rise for about an hour, or until it has doubled in size.

4 Knock back the dough by gently kneading for about a minute, then divide into two balls. To roll out the dough, flatten each ball, then, using a rolling pin, roll out on a lightly floured work surface, giving a quarter turn between each roll.

5 Preheat the oven to 220°C/425°F/Gas Mark 7. Place the pizza bases on two baking trays, using a rolling pin to transfer them from the work surface.

6 Heat the oil in a griddle pan over a medium heat. Add the garlic and courgette and cook over a medium heat for 4–5 minutes, turning regularly, until softened and chargrilled. Remove with a slotted spoon and drain on kitchen paper.

7 Divide the passata between the two pizza bases, spreading almost to the edges. Place the courgette slices on the pizza bases, scatter with the cheese and season to taste with salt and pepper. Bake in the preheated oven for 10–12 minutes, or until the cheese is turning golden and the bases are crisp underneath. Garnish with the fresh mint and serve immediately.

NEW POTATO, FETA & HERB FRITTATA

Serves: 4

Prep: 20 mins, plus cooling

Cook: 35–40 mins

Ingredients

250 g/9 oz new potatoes, scrubbed

85 g/3 oz baby spinach leaves

5 eggs

1 tbsp chopped fresh dill, plus extra to garnish

1 tbsp snipped fresh chives, plus extra to garnish

115 g/4 oz vegetarian feta cheese, crumbled

10 g/¼ oz butter

1 tbsp olive oil

salt and pepper

Method

1 Bring a saucepan of lightly salted water to the boil, add the potatoes, bring back to the boil and cook for 25 minutes until tender. Place the spinach in a colander and drain the potatoes over the top to wilt the spinach. Set aside until cool enough to handle.

2 Cut the potatoes lengthways into 5-mm/¼-inch thick slices. Squeeze the excess water from the spinach leaves. Preheat the grill to high.

3 Lightly beat the eggs, dill and chives together. Season with pepper and add 85 g/3 oz of the cheese. Heat the butter and oil in a 20-cm/8-inch frying pan until melted and foaming. Add the potato slices and spinach and cook, stirring, for 1 minute. Pour the egg and cheese mixture over the top.

4 Cook, stirring, over a moderate heat for 1 minute until half set, then continue to cook for a further 2–3 minutes, without stirring, until set and golden brown underneath. Sprinkle the remaining cheese over the top, place under the preheated grill and cook for 2 minutes until golden brown on top. Serve hot or cold, sprinkled with chives and dill.

FAMILY FAVOURITES

PARSNIP LAYERED CASSEROLE

Serves: 4–6 **Prep: 20 mins** **Cook: 55–60 mins**

Ingredients

3 tbsp olive oil

600 g/1 lb 5 oz parsnips, thinly sliced

1 tsp fresh thyme leaves

1 tsp caster sugar

300 ml/10 fl oz double cream

600 g/1 lb 5 oz tomatoes, thinly sliced

1 tsp dried oregano

150 g/5½ oz vegetarian Cheddar cheese, grated

salt and pepper

Method

1 Preheat the oven to 180°C/350°F/Gas Mark 4.

2 Heat the oil in a frying pan over a medium heat, add the parsnips, thyme, sugar and salt and pepper to taste and cook, stirring frequently, for 6–8 minutes until golden and softened.

3 Spread half the parsnips over the base of a gratin dish. Pour over half the cream, then arrange half the tomatoes in an even layer across the parsnips. Season to taste with salt and pepper and scatter over half the oregano. Sprinkle over half the Cheddar cheese. Top with the remaining parsnips and tomatoes. Sprinkle with the remaining oregano, season to taste with salt and pepper and pour over the remaining cream. Scatter over the remaining cheese.

4 Cover with foil and bake in the preheated oven for 40 minutes, or until the parsnips are tender. Remove the foil and return to the oven for a further 5–10 minutes until the top is golden and bubbling. Serve immediately.

FAMILY FAVOURITES

RIGATONI WITH ROAST COURGETTE & TOMATO SAUCE

Serves: 4 **Prep: 20 mins** **Cook: 30–35 mins**

Ingredients

4 courgettes, roughly chopped

2½ tbsp olive oil

1 onion, finely chopped

1 garlic clove, crushed

800 g/1 lb 12 oz canned chopped tomatoes

6 sun-dried tomatoes, chopped

225 ml/8 fl oz vegetable stock

½ tsp dried oregano

280 g/10 oz dried rigatoni pasta

125 g/4½ oz vegetarian mascarpone cheese

salt and pepper

large handful of fresh basil leaves, torn into pieces

Method

1 Preheat the oven to 200°C/400°F/Gas Mark 6. Place the courgettes and 1½ tablespoons of the oil in a large ovenproof dish. Toss together and spread out in a single layer. Roast in the preheated oven for 15–20 minutes until tender and lightly browned.

2 Meanwhile, heat the remaining oil in a saucepan. Add the onion and garlic and cook very gently for 5 minutes until soft. Add the canned tomatoes, sun-dried tomatoes, stock and oregano. Simmer for 10 minutes until the liquid has reduced slightly.

3 Bring a large saucepan of lightly salted water to the boil. Add the rigatoni, bring back to the boil and cook for 11–13 minutes, or until tender but still firm to the bite. Drain well, then return to the pan.

4 Add the mascarpone cheese to the hot sauce and stir until melted and smooth. Season well with salt and pepper. Add to the pasta with the roasted courgettes and the basil leaves. Toss together until the pasta is well coated in sauce. Serve immediately.

ROAST BUTTERNUT SQUASH

Serves: 4

Prep: 25–30 mins, plus cooling

Cook: 1 hour 10 mins

Ingredients

1 butternut squash, about 450 g/1 lb

1 onion, chopped

2–3 garlic cloves, crushed

4 small tomatoes, chopped

85 g/3 oz chestnut mushrooms, chopped

85 g/3 oz canned butter beans, drained, rinsed and roughly chopped

1 courgette, about 115 g/4 oz, trimmed and grated

1 tbsp chopped fresh oregano, plus extra to garnish

2 tbsp tomato purée

300 ml/10 fl oz water

4 spring onions, chopped

1 tbsp vegetarian Worcestershire or hot pepper sauce, or to taste

pepper

Method

1 Preheat the oven to 190°C/375°F/Gas Mark 5. Prick the squash all over with a metal skewer then roast for 40 minutes, or until tender. Remove from the oven and leave until cool enough to handle.

2 Cut the squash in half, scoop out and discard the seeds then scoop out some of the flesh, making hollows in both halves. Chop the cooked flesh and put in a bowl. Place the two halves side by side in a large roasting tin.

3 Add the onion, garlic, chopped tomatoes and mushrooms to the cooked squash flesh. Add the roughly chopped butter beans, grated courgette, chopped oregano and pepper to taste and mix well. Spoon the filling into the two halves of the squash, packing it down as firmly as possible.

4 Mix the tomato purée with the water, spring onions and Worcestershire sauce in a small bowl and pour around the squash.

5 Cover loosely with a large sheet of foil and bake for 30 minutes, or until piping hot. Serve, divided equally between four warmed plates, garnished with extra chopped oregano.

PENNE IN TOMATO SAUCE WITH TWO CHEESES

Serves: 4　　　**Prep: 15 mins**　　　**Cook: 30–35 mins**

Ingredients

450 g/1 lb dried penne

115 g/4 oz vegetarian mozzarella cheese, diced

55 g/2 oz freshly grated vegetarian Parmesan-style cheese

Tomato sauce

25 g/1 oz butter

2 tbsp olive oil

2 shallots, finely chopped

2 garlic cloves, finely chopped

1 celery stick, finely chopped

400 g/14 oz canned chopped tomatoes

2 tbsp tomato purée

brown sugar, to taste

1 tsp dried oregano

100 ml/3½ fl oz water

salt and pepper

Method

1 For the tomato sauce, melt the butter with the oil in a saucepan. Add the shallots, garlic and celery and cook over a low heat, stirring occasionally, for 5 minutes, until softened. Stir in the tomatoes, tomato purée, sugar to taste, oregano and water and season to taste with salt and pepper. Increase the heat to medium and bring to the boil, then reduce the heat and simmer, stirring occasionally, for 15–20 minutes, until thickened.

2 Meanwhile, bring a large, heavy-based saucepan of lightly salted water to the boil. Add the penne, bring back to the boil and cook for 8–10 minutes, or until just tender but still firm to the bite. Drain and return to the pan.

3 Add the tomato sauce and the cheeses to the pasta and toss well over a very low heat until the cheeses have melted. Transfer to a serving dish and serve immediately.

BEAN & TOMATO CASSEROLE WITH PARMESAN TOASTS

Serves: 4

Prep: 15–20 mins, plus overnight soaking

Cook: 1 hour 35 mins– 1 hour 50 mins

Ingredients

350 g/12 oz borlotti beans, soaked overnight

4 tbsp extra virgin olive oil, plus extra for drizzling

25 g/1 oz butter

1 large onion, thinly sliced

15–20 fresh sage leaves, sliced

2 large garlic cloves, thinly sliced

1 tbsp tomato purée

800 g/1 lb 12 oz canned chopped tomatoes

300 ml/10 fl oz vegetable stock

4 tbsp chopped fresh flat-leaf parsley

50 g/1¾ oz coarsely grated vegetarian Parmesan-style cheese

8 thin slices ciabatta, toasted

sea salt and pepper

small fresh sage sprigs, to garnish

Method

1 Drain the beans, rinse well and put them into a large saucepan. Cover with water and bring to the boil. Boil for 10 minutes, then reduce the heat and simmer for 45–60 minutes, or until tender. Drain.

2 Heat the oil and butter in a large saucepan over a medium heat. Add the onion and sage and fry for 5 minutes, until the onion is translucent. Add the garlic and fry for 2 minutes, until just coloured. Add the tomato purée and fry for 1 minute, stirring.

3 Stir in the tomatoes, beans and stock and season with salt and pepper. Bring to the boil, then reduce the heat and simmer, partially covered, for 20 minutes. Add the parsley and half the cheese.

4 Ladle the beans into shallow soup plates. Top each plate with 2 slices of toasted ciabatta. Drizzle the bread with the remaining oil and sprinkle with the remaining cheese. Garnish with sage sprigs and serve immediately.

★ **Variation**

For a quicker version of this recipe use a can of borlotti beans.

FAMILY FAVOURITES

SPECIAL OCCASIONS

SPICED PARSNIP GRATIN WITH GINGER CREAM 158

JERUSALEM ARTICHOKE & HAZELNUT GRATIN 160

BAKED GNOCCHI WITH TOMATO SAUCE 162

CREAMED MORELS ON SPINACH & POLENTA CROÛTONS 164

MIXED NUT ROAST WITH CRANBERRY & RED WINE SAUCE 166

CARROT TARTE TATIN 168

BABY SQUASH WITH FREEKEH STUFFING 169

SWEETCORN, CHILLI & TORTILLA GRATIN 170

FENNEL RISOTTO WITH VODKA 172

WILD MUSHROOM RISOTTO 174

CHARD & RICOTTA FILO PIE 176

MUSHROOM & WALNUT OPEN TART 178

PUMPKIN & GRUYÈRE STEW 179

QUINOA-STUFFED AUBERGINES 180

ROASTED SQUASH & CELERIAC WITH BALSAMIC GLAZE 181

MOROCCAN VEGETABLES 182

POTATO GNOCCHI WITH WALNUT PESTO 184

SPROUTING BROCCOLI WITH CAPER BUTTER SAUCE 186

PUMPKIN & CHESTNUT RISOTTO 188

TOMATO SOUFFLÉ 190

RED CABBAGE STUFFED WITH MUSHROOMS, NUTS & RICE 192

KALE & BUTTER BEAN CASSEROLE 194

CARAMELIZED ONION TART 196

COURGETTE & BASIL RISOTTO 197

ROAST BEETROOT PARCELS WITH HORSERADISH BUTTER 198

TOFU MOUSSAKA 200

VEGETARIAN PAELLA 202

SQUASH, KALE & FARRO STEW 204

SPICED PARSNIP GRATIN WITH GINGER CREAM

Serves: 4   **Prep: 15 mins**   **Cook: 45–50 mins**

Ingredients

butter, for greasing

3 large parsnips, about 750 g/1 lb 10 oz, thinly sliced

425 ml/15 fl oz double cream

250 ml/9 fl oz vegetable stock

1 garlic clove, crushed

2.5-cm/1-inch piece fresh ginger, roughly chopped and crushed in a garlic press

¼ tsp freshly ground white pepper

⅛ tsp freshly grated nutmeg, plus extra to garnish

sea salt

snipped chives, to garnish

Method

1 Lightly grease a large gratin dish. Place the parsnips in a steamer basket set over a saucepan of boiling water. Steam for 3 minutes, until barely tender, shaking halfway through cooking. Tip into the prepared dish and lightly season with salt.

2 Preheat the oven to 180°C/350°F/Gas Mark 4. Gently heat the cream and stock in a saucepan with the garlic and ginger. Do not allow the mixture to boil. Add the pepper, nutmeg and sea salt to taste.

3 Pour the hot cream mixture over the parsnips. Cover the dish with foil and bake in the preheated oven for 20 minutes, with an oven tray underneath to catch any drips.

4 Remove the foil and bake for a further 15–20 minutes, until golden on top. Sprinkle with a little more nutmeg and some chives and serve immediately.

★ Variation

For a crunchy topping, sprinkle a fine layer of breadcrumbs and vegetarian Parmesan-style cheese over the top.

JERUSALEM ARTICHOKE & HAZELNUT GRATIN

Serves: 4

Prep: 20 mins,
plus cooling

Cook: 45–55 mins

Ingredients

750 g/1 lb 10 oz Jerusalem artichokes

squeeze of lemon juice

4 tbsp skinned hazelnuts, roughly chopped

40 g/1½ oz coarse ciabatta breadcrumbs

25 g/1 oz butter, plus extra for greasing

salt and pepper

steamed French beans, to serve

Garlic cream

250 ml/9 fl oz whipping cream

7 large garlic cloves, lightly crushed

sliver of lemon peel

squeeze of lemon juice

Method

1 To make the garlic cream, heat the cream, garlic and lemon peel in a saucepan over a medium heat, then simmer for about 5 minutes, until slightly reduced. Remove from the heat and leave to stand in a warm place.

2 Peel the artichokes, dropping them into water with a squeeze of lemon juice. Cut in half if they are large. Place in a steamer basket set over a saucepan of boiling water and steam for 8–10 minutes, until just tender at the edges. Leave to cool, then slice fairly thickly.

3 Strain the garlic cream into a jug. Add the lemon juice and season to taste.

4 Preheat the oven to 190°C/375°F/Gas Mark 5. Grease a 2-litre/3½-pint baking dish with butter. Arrange half the artichoke slices in the base of the prepared dish. Season with salt and pepper. Sprinkle with the nuts, then top with the remaining artichokes and a little more seasoning.

5 Pour over the warm garlic cream. Sprinkle with the breadcrumbs and dot with the butter.

6 Bake in the preheated oven for 30–35 minutes, until the artichokes are tender and the topping is golden and bubbling. Serve hot with steamed French beans.

SPECIAL OCCASIONS

BAKED GNOCCHI WITH TOMATO SAUCE

Serves: 4

Prep: 25 mins,
plus chilling

Cook: 1 hour 5 mins–
1 hour 15 mins

Ingredients

4 egg yolks

2 tsp granulated sugar

55 g/2 oz plain flour

2 tbsp cornflour

pinch of salt

55 g/2 oz butter, melted,
plus extra for greasing

115 g/4 oz vegetarian
Parmesan-style cheese,
grated

425 ml/15 fl oz milk

Tomato sauce

25 g/1 oz butter

2 tbsp olive oil

1 onion, finely chopped

2 garlic cloves, finely
chopped

1 celery stick, finely
chopped

800 g/1 lb 12 oz canned
chopped tomatoes

2 tbsp tomato purée

brown sugar, to taste

1 tbsp dry vermouth

1 tbsp chopped fresh
flat-leaf parsley, plus extra
to garnish

5 tbsp water

salt and pepper

Method

1 To make the gnocchi, whisk the egg yolks with the granulated sugar in a saucepan until pale and creamy. Sift the flour, cornflour and salt into a bowl, then gradually beat into the egg yolk mixture. Stir in the melted butter and 85 g/3 oz of the cheese. Set the pan over a medium heat and gradually stir in the milk. Cook, stirring constantly, for 3–4 minutes, until thick and smooth. Remove the pan from the heat and turn out the mixture onto a baking sheet rinsed with cold water. Spread out to a thickness of 1 cm/½ inch and smooth the surface. Chill in the refrigerator for 30 minutes.

2 Meanwhile, make the sauce. Melt the butter with the oil in a saucepan. Add the onion, garlic and celery and cook over a low heat, stirring occasionally, for 5 minutes, until softened. Stir in the tomatoes, tomato purée, brown sugar to taste, vermouth, parsley and water and season to taste with salt and pepper. Increase the heat to medium and bring to the boil, then reduce the heat and simmer, stirring occasionally, for 25–30 minutes, until thickened.

3 Preheat the oven to 190°C/375°F/Gas Mark 5. Grease an ovenproof dish with butter. Cut the gnocchi into 3–4-cm/1¼–1½-inch squares and put them into the prepared dish, slightly overlapping. Bake in the preheated oven for 15 minutes. Pour the tomato sauce over the top and bake for a further 5–10 minutes, until hot. Sprinkle with the remaining cheese, garnish with parsley and serve immediately.

CREAMED MORELS ON SPINACH & POLENTA CROÛTONS

Serves: 4–6

Prep: 25 mins, plus cooling

Cook: 20–25 mins

Ingredients

6 handfuls fresh morels

3 tbsp olive oil

4 shallots, finely chopped

2 garlic cloves, crushed

100 ml/3½ fl oz Marsala

200 ml/7 fl oz double cream

2 tbsp wholegrain mustard

1 small bunch fresh tarragon, finely chopped, plus extra to garnish

salt and pepper

Polenta croûtons

1 litre/1¾ pints vegetable stock

250 g/9 oz quick-cook polenta

olive oil, for greasing

100 g/3½ oz freshly grated vegetarian Parmesan-style cheese

2 handfuls baby spinach, roughly torn

2 tsp coarsely cracked black peppercorns

100 g/3½ oz butter, softened

salt and pepper

Method

1 To make the croûtons, pour the stock into a large saucepan and bring to a rolling boil. Add the polenta in a steady stream, stirring quickly with a large balloon whisk. Cook according to the packet instructions. Lightly grease an oven dish.

2 Use a wooden spoon to stir the cheese, spinach, peppercorns and half the butter into the polenta. Taste and adjust the seasoning, if necessary.

3 Pour out the polenta mixture into the prepared dish, smooth with a palette knife and leave to cool. When the polenta has set, use a 10-cm/ 4-inch round pastry cutter to cut out the required number of rounds.

4 Cut the morels in half and gently wash them, taking care to remove any traces of soil and grit. Dry gently with kitchen paper. Heat the oil in a saucepan over a medium heat, add the shallots and garlic and cook for 3–4 minutes, until soft.

5 Add the morels and cook, stirring constantly, for 2 minutes. Pour in the Marsala and bubble briefly, then add the cream, mustard and tarragon. Season to taste with salt and pepper. Keep warm.

6 Heat the remaining butter in a frying pan over a high heat, add the polenta croûtons and cook for 3–4 minutes on each side until crisp and golden. Serve the croûtons immediately, heaped with the creamed morels and garnished with tarragon.

MIXED NUT ROAST WITH CRANBERRY & RED WINE SAUCE

Serves: 4   **Prep: 20 mins**   **Cook: 35 mins**

Ingredients

2 tbsp butter, plus extra for greasing

2 garlic cloves, chopped

1 large onion, chopped

50 g/1¾ oz pine nuts, toasted

75 g/2¾ oz hazelnuts, toasted

50 g/1¾ oz ground walnuts

50 g/1¾ oz ground cashew nuts

100 g/3½ oz wholemeal breadcrumbs

1 egg, lightly beaten

2 tbsp chopped fresh thyme

250 ml/9 fl oz vegetable stock

salt and pepper

sprigs of fresh thyme, to garnish

Cranberry & red wine sauce

175 g/6 oz fresh cranberries

100 g/3½ oz caster sugar

300 ml/10 fl oz vegetarian red wine

1 cinnamon stick

Method

1 Preheat the oven to 180°C/350°F/Gas Mark 4. Grease a 450-g/1-lb loaf tin and line it with greaseproof paper.

2 Melt the butter in a saucepan over a medium heat. Add the garlic and onion and cook, stirring, for about 3 minutes. Remove the pan from the heat.

3 Grind the pine nuts and hazelnuts in a mortar with a pestle. Stir into the pan with the walnuts and cashew nuts and add the breadcrumbs, egg, thyme, stock and seasoning.

4 Spoon the mixture into the loaf tin and level the surface. Cook in the centre of the preheated oven for 30 minutes or until cooked through and golden. Insert a skewer into the centre of the loaf – it's cooked if the skewer comes out clean.

5 Halfway through the cooking time, make the sauce. Put all the ingredients into a saucepan and bring to the boil. Reduce the heat and simmer, stirring occasionally, for 15 minutes.

6 Remove the nut roast from the oven and turn out onto a serving platter. Garnish the roast with sprigs of thyme and serve with the cranberry and red wine sauce.

SPECIAL OCCASIONS

CARROT TARTE TATIN

Serves: 4 **Prep: 20 mins** **Cook: 45–50 mins**

Ingredients

600 g/1 lb 5 oz young carrots, cut into 2.5-cm/ 1-inch chunks

2 tbsp clear honey

25 g/1 oz butter

1 small bunch fresh thyme, chopped

350 g/12 oz ready-made puff pastry, thawed if frozen

plain flour, for dusting

salt and pepper

Method

1 Bring a large saucepan of lightly salted water to the boil. Add the carrots, bring back to the boil and cook for 10–15 minutes, until just tender. Drain, toss with the honey, butter and thyme and season to taste with salt and pepper.

2 Preheat the oven to 200°C/400°F/Gas Mark 6. Spoon the carrots over the base of a 20-cm/8-inch tarte tatin tin or round cake tin with a depth of about 3 cm/1¼ inches. Roast in the preheated oven for 15 minutes, or until the carrots are caramelized. Remove the tin from the oven but leave the oven on.

3 Roll out the pastry on a floured work surface into a round large enough to fit the tin and give a 2-cm/¾-inch overlap. Lay the pastry carefully over the carrots and tuck the edges down between the carrots and the side of the tin to make a border. Bake in the oven for 15 minutes, or until the pastry is puffed and golden.

4 Remove the tart from the oven and turn the tin over onto a plate to release. Cut the tart into slices and serve immediately.

SPECIAL OCCASIONS

Serves: 4 **Prep: 25–30 mins** **Cook: 1 hour 10 mins–1 hour 15 mins**

Ingredients

115 g/4 oz freekeh, rinsed

350 ml/12 fl oz water

1½ tbsp tomato purée

4 round baby squash, about 10 cm/4 inches in diameter

3 tbsp olive oil, plus extra for oiling and drizzling

1 onion, finely chopped

2 garlic cloves, finely chopped

40 g/1½ oz walnut halves, roughly chopped

80 g/2¾ oz canned black beans, drained and rinsed

4 tbsp chopped fresh flat-leaf parsley

115 g/4 oz vegetarian halloumi cheese, sliced

salt and pepper

Method

1 Put the freekeh into a saucepan with the water, tomato purée and ½ teaspoon of salt. Bring to the boil, cover and simmer for 25 minutes, then drain and set aside.

2 Preheat the oven to 200°C/400°F/Gas Mark 6. Lightly oil a roasting tin. Slice the top third off the squash and scoop out the seeds.

3 Heat the 3 tablespoons of oil in a frying pan, add the onion and fry over a medium heat for 3 minutes. Add the garlic, walnuts and beans and fry for a further 2 minutes. Tip into a bowl. Stir in the reserved freekeh and the parsley and season to taste with salt and pepper. Spoon the mixture into the squash, packing it in well.

4 Place the squash in the prepared tin. Cover the tin with a thick layer of aluminium foil, sealing well, and roast in the preheated oven for 30 minutes. Remove from the oven and increase the oven temperature to 220°C/425°F/Gas Mark 7.

5 Arrange the halloumi on top of the squash and drizzle with a little oil. Return to the oven and roast, uncovered, for a further 5–8 minutes, until the cheese is slightly browned. Serve immediately.

SPECIAL OCCASIONS

SWEETCORN, CHILLI & TORTILLA GRATIN

Serves: 4–6   **Prep: 30 mins**   **Cook: 1 hour 10 mins–1 hour 15 mins**

Ingredients

groundnut oil, for greasing and frying

6 corn cobs, with husks

2 green peppers

2–3 green chillies

6 corn tortillas, sliced into 2.5-cm/1-inch strips

225 g/8 oz vegetarian Cheddar cheese, coarsely grated

2 tbsp chopped fresh coriander, to garnish

Tomato sauce

8–10 tomatoes

1 onion, sliced into thick rings

3 garlic cloves

sea salt and pepper

Method

1 Preheat the oven to 190°C/375°F/Gas Mark 5. Preheat the grill to high. Grease a 2-litre/3½-pint ovenproof dish.

2 Place the sweetcorn under the hot grill and cook, turning, for 10 minutes. Discard the husks. Slice off the kernels and reserve.

3 Place the green peppers and chillies under the hot grill and cook until blackened. Discard the skins and seeds. Roughly chop the flesh and reserve.

4 To make the tomato sauce, place the tomatoes, onion and garlic under the hot grill and cook until blackened. Remove the tomato stalks but not the skins. Transfer to a food processor and process to a chunky purée.

5 Heat 2 tablespoons of oil in a frying pan. Stir in the tomato mixture and simmer for 10 minutes, until thickened. Season with salt and pepper, then pour into a large bowl.

6 Heat 5 mm/¼ inch of oil in a large frying pan over a medium–high heat. Add the tortilla strips, in batches, and fry for 2–3 minutes, until crisp. Drain on kitchen paper. Stir into the tomato mixture, mixing well.

7 Arrange one third of the tortilla strips in the prepared dish. Sprinkle with half the green pepper mixture, half the corn and one third of the cheese. Season with salt and pepper.

8 Add another layer of tortilla strips, the remaining corn and green pepper mixture and half the remaining cheese. Season again, then add the rest of the tortilla strips and cheese. Bake in the preheated oven for 30 minutes, until golden. Sprinkle with the chopped coriander and serve hot.

FENNEL RISOTTO WITH VODKA

Serves: 4–5　　　**Prep: 20 mins**　　　**Cook: 30–35 mins,**
plus standing

Ingredients

2 large fennel bulbs

2 tbsp vegetable oil

80 g/2¾ oz unsalted butter

1 large onion, finely chopped

350 g/12 oz risotto rice

150 ml/5 fl oz vodka or lemon-flavoured vodka

1.3 litres/2¼ pints hot vegetable stock

55 g/2 oz freshly grated vegetarian Parmesan-style cheese

5–6 tbsp lemon juice

Method

1 Trim the fennel, reserving the fronds to garnish. Cut the bulbs in half lengthways, remove the V-shaped cores and roughly chop the flesh.

2 Heat the oil and half the butter in a large, heavy-based saucepan over a medium heat. Add the onion and fennel and cook for about 2 minutes, stirring frequently, until soft.

3 Add the rice and cook for about 2 minutes, stirring frequently, or until the rice is translucent and well coated.

4 Pour the vodka into the saucepan. It will bubble rapidly and evaporate almost immediately. Add a ladleful of the hot stock. Cook, stirring constantly, until all the stock has been absorbed.

5 Continue stirring in the stock, about half a ladleful at a time, allowing each addition to be absorbed by the rice before adding the next. Cook for 20–25 minutes, or until all the liquid is absorbed and the rice is creamy.

6 Stir in the remaining butter, the grated cheese and lemon juice. Remove from the heat, cover and leave to stand for 1 minute before serving.

7 Garnish with a few of the reserved fennel fronds, and serve immediately.

WILD MUSHROOM RISOTTO

Serves: 6

Prep: 20 mins,
plus soaking

Cook: 30–35 mins

Ingredients

55 g/2 oz dried porcini or morel mushrooms

about 500 g/1 lb 2 oz mixed fresh wild mushrooms, such as porcini, field mushrooms and chanterelles, halved if large

4 tbsp olive oil

3–4 garlic cloves, finely chopped

55 g/2 oz butter

1 onion, finely chopped

350 g/12 oz risotto rice

50 ml/2 fl oz dry white vermouth

1.2 litres/2 pints simmering chicken or vegetable stock

115 g/4 oz freshly grated vegetarian Parmesan-style cheese

4 tbsp chopped fresh flat-leaf parsley

salt and pepper

Method

1 Place the dried mushrooms in a heatproof bowl and add boiling water to cover. Set aside to soak for 30 minutes, then carefully lift out and pat dry. Strain the soaking liquid through a sieve lined with kitchen paper and set aside.

2 Trim the fresh mushrooms and gently brush clean. Heat 3 tablespoons of the oil in a large frying pan. Add the fresh mushrooms and stir-fry for 1–2 minutes. Add the garlic and the soaked mushrooms and cook, stirring frequently, for 2 minutes. Transfer to a plate.

3 Heat the remaining oil and half the butter in a large heavy-based saucepan. Add the onion and cook over a medium heat, stirring occasionally, for 2 minutes, until softened. Reduce the heat, stir in the rice and cook, stirring constantly, for 2–3 minutes, until the grains are translucent. Add the vermouth and cook, stirring, for 1 minute until reduced.

4 Gradually add the hot stock, a ladleful at a time, until all the liquid is absorbed and the rice is creamy. Add half the reserved mushroom soaking liquid to the risotto and stir in the mushrooms. Season to taste and add more mushroom liquid, if necessary. Remove the pan from the heat and stir in the remaining butter, grated cheese and chopped parsley. Serve.

SPECIAL OCCASIONS

CHARD & RICOTTA FILO PIE

Serves: 9   **Prep: 35 mins**   **Cook: 45–50 mins**

Ingredients

900 g/2 lb rainbow chard

55 g/2 oz butter

2 leeks, sliced

2 garlic cloves, thinly sliced

3 tbsp chopped mixed fresh herbs, such as thyme, marjoram and flat-leaf parsley

400 g/14 oz vegetarian ricotta cheese

55 g/2 oz freshly grated vegetarian Parmesan-style cheese

⅛ tsp freshly grated nutmeg

2 eggs, beaten

12 large sheets filo pastry

olive oil, for brushing

55 g/2 oz pine nuts

sea salt and pepper

Method

1 Chop the chard stems into chunks. Slice the leaves into thin ribbons.

2 Heat the butter in a large frying pan over a medium heat. Add the leeks and chard stalks, cover and fry for 5–7 minutes, until soft.

3 Add the chard leaves, garlic and herbs. Cover and gently fry until the leaves are tender. Tip the vegetables into a colander and drain.

4 Beat together the ricotta cheese, Parmesan-style cheese, nutmeg and eggs in a large bowl. Mix in the drained vegetables. Season with salt and pepper.

5 Preheat the oven to 190°C/375°F/Gas Mark 5. Place 1 sheet of filo pastry in a greased 23 x 30-cm/9 x 12-inch roasting tin, trimming to fit as necessary. Brush with oil and sprinkle with a few pine nuts. Add 5 more sheets, lightly brushing each one with oil and sprinkling with pine nuts.

6 Pour in the filling and level the surface. Cover with 5 more sheets of filo pastry, brushing each sheet with oil and sprinkling with pine nuts. Add the final sheet and brush with oil.

7 Using a sharp knife, cut through all the pastry and filling layers to make
   7.5-cm/3-inch squares. Bake in the preheated oven for 35–40 minutes, until
   golden and crisp. Serve hot or at room temperature.

MUSHROOM & WALNUT OPEN TART

Serves: 4   **Prep: 20 mins**   **Cook: 30–40 mins**

Ingredients

1 tbsp olive oil

15 g/½ oz butter

1 red onion, sliced

1 garlic clove, crushed

500 g/1 lb 2 oz closed-cup chestnut mushrooms, sliced

85 g/3 oz walnuts, chopped

2 tbsp chopped fresh flat-leaf parsley, plus extra to garnish

500 g/1 lb 2 oz ready-made shortcrust pastry

plain flour, for dusting

beaten egg, for glazing

salt and pepper

Method

1 Preheat the oven to 200°C/400°F/Gas Mark 6. Heat the oil and butter in a large frying pan, add the onion and stir-fry for 2–3 minutes until soft, but not brown.

2 Add the garlic and mushrooms and cook, stirring, for 3–4 minutes until soft. Cook until any liquid has evaporated, then remove from the heat and stir in the walnuts, parsley, and salt and pepper to taste.

3 Roll out the pastry on a lightly floured work surface to a 35-cm/14-inch round and place on a large baking sheet. Pile the mushroom mixture onto the pastry, leaving a 9-cm/3½-inch border around the edge.

4 Lift the edges of the pastry and tuck up around the filling, leaving an open centre. Brush the pastry with beaten egg to glaze.

5 Bake in the preheated oven for 25–30 minutes until the pastry is golden brown. Serve warm, sprinkled with parsley.

SPECIAL OCCASIONS

PUMPKIN & GRUYÈRE STEW

Serves: 4-6   **Prep: 20–25 mins**   **Cook: 1 hour 15 mins**

Ingredients

1 large pumpkin

300 ml/10 fl oz double cream

3 garlic cloves, thinly sliced

1 tbsp fresh thyme leaves

125 g/4½ oz vegetarian Gruyère cheese, grated

salt and pepper

crusty bread, to serve

Method

1 Preheat the oven to 180°C/350°F/Gas Mark 4.

2 Cut horizontally straight through the top quarter of the pumpkin to form a lid. Scoop out the seeds. Put the pumpkin in a large, deep ovenproof dish. Heat together the cream and garlic in a saucepan until just below boiling point. Remove from the heat, season to taste with salt and pepper and stir in the thyme. Pour into the pumpkin and pop the lid on top.

3 Bake in the preheated oven for 1 hour, or until the flesh is tender – the exact cooking time will depend on the size of the pumpkin. Take care not to overcook the pumpkin, or it may collapse. Remove from the oven, lift off the lid and scatter over the Gruyère cheese. Return to the oven and bake for a further 10 minutes.

4 Serve the soft pumpkin flesh with a generous portion of the cheesy cream and crusty bread.

SPECIAL OCCASIONS

QUINOA-STUFFED AUBERGINES

Serves: 2

Prep: 25 mins, plus cooling

Cook: 40–45 mins

Ingredients

2 aubergines (about 950 g/
2 lb 2 oz in total)

1 tbsp olive oil

1 small onion, diced

2 garlic cloves, finely
chopped

135 g/4¾ oz white quinoa,
rinsed

350 ml/12 fl oz vegetable
stock

1 tsp salt

pinch of pepper

2 tbsp flaked almonds,
toasted

3 tbsp finely chopped
fresh mint

85 g/3 oz vegetarian feta
cheese, crumbled

Method

1 Preheat the oven to 230°C/450°F/Gas Mark 8.
Place the aubergines on a baking tray and bake
in the preheated oven for 15 minutes, or until soft.
Remove from the oven and leave to cool slightly.

2 Meanwhile, heat the oil in a large, heavy-based
frying pan over a medium–high heat. Add the
onion and garlic and cook, stirring occasionally,
for about 5 minutes, or until soft. Add the quinoa,
stock, salt and pepper.

3 Cut each aubergine in half lengthways and
scoop out the flesh, leaving a 5-mm/¼-inch thick
border inside the skin so they hold their shape.

4 Chop the aubergine flesh and stir it into the
quinoa mixture in the frying pan. Reduce the
heat to low–medium, cover and cook for about
15 minutes, or until the quinoa is cooked through.
Remove from the heat and stir in the flaked
almonds, 2 tablespoons of the mint and half
the cheese.

5 Divide the quinoa mixture equally between
the aubergine skins and top with the remaining
cheese. Bake for about 10–15 minutes, or until
the cheese is bubbling and beginning to brown.
Garnish with the remaining mint and serve.

SPECIAL OCCASIONS

ROASTED SQUASH & CELERIAC WITH BALSAMIC GLAZE

Serves: 2–3   **Prep: 20 mins**   **Cook: 30 mins**

Ingredients

1 kg/2 lb 4 oz dense-fleshed squash, such as Kabocha or Crown Prince

½ celeriac, peeled

5 tbsp rapeseed oil

1 tbsp thick balsamic vinegar

1 tsp coriander seeds, crushed

1 tsp fresh thyme leaves

25 g/1 oz butter

sea salt flakes and pepper

steamed broccoli or green cabbage, to serve

Method

1 Preheat the oven to 200°C/400°F/Gas Mark 6. Slice the squash into quarters. Cut away the peel and scoop out the seeds. Cut each quarter crossways into two pieces. Cut the celeriac into quarters and then into chunks smaller than the squash pieces.

2 Whisk together the oil, vinegar, coriander seeds and thyme with some pepper and a good pinch of salt in a large bowl. Add the squash and celeriac, turning in the mixture until well coated.

3 Tip the vegetables into a large roasting tray and spread out in a single layer. Dot with the butter.

4 Roast in the preheated oven for 30 minutes, turning every 10 minutes or so, until tender and slightly blackened.

5 Serve immediately with steamed broccoli.

SPECIAL OCCASIONS

MOROCCAN VEGETABLES

Serves: 4 **Prep: 20–25 mins** **Cook: 50 mins**

Ingredients

4 tomatoes, peeled and deseeded

700 ml/1¼ pints vegetable stock

1 onion, sliced

2 carrots, sliced diagonally

1 tbsp chopped fresh coriander

175 g/6 oz courgettes, sliced

1 small turnip, cubed

½ tsp ground turmeric

¼ tsp ground ginger

¼ tsp ground cinnamon

400 g/14 oz canned chickpeas, drained and rinsed

225 g/8 oz couscous

salt

fresh coriander sprigs, to garnish

Method

1 Roughly chop the tomatoes and reserve half. Place the remainder in a blender or food processor and process until a smooth purée forms. Transfer to a large saucepan and add 400 ml/14 fl oz of the vegetable stock. Bring to the boil, then reduce the heat and add the onion, carrots, chopped fresh coriander and salt to taste. Simmer, stirring occasionally, for 10 minutes.

2 Stir in the courgettes, turnip, reserved tomatoes, turmeric, ginger and cinnamon. Partially cover and simmer for a further 30 minutes. Stir in the chickpeas and simmer.

3 Meanwhile, bring the remaining vegetable stock to the boil in a heavy-based saucepan. Add a pinch of salt, then sprinkle in the couscous, stirring constantly. Remove the saucepan from the heat, cover with a tight-fitting lid and leave to stand for 5 minutes. Fluff up the couscous with a fork and divide among four serving bowls. Top with the moroccan vegetables and serve garnished with coriander sprigs.

POTATO GNOCCHI WITH WALNUT PESTO

Serves: 4

Prep: 30 mins, plus cooling

Cook: 44–45 mins

Ingredients

450 g/1 lb floury potatoes, washed but not peeled

55 g/2 oz freshly grated vegetarian Parmesan-style cheese

1 egg, beaten

200 g/7 oz plain flour, plus extra for dusting

salt and pepper

Walnut pesto

40 g/1½ oz fresh flat-leaf parsley, chopped

2 tbsp capers, rinsed and chopped

2 garlic cloves, chopped

175 ml/6 fl oz extra virgin olive oil

70 g/2½ oz walnut pieces

40 g/1½ oz freshly grated vegetarian Parmesan-style cheese

salt and pepper

Method

1. Bring a large saucepan of lightly salted water to the boil. Add the potatoes, bring back to the boil and cook for 30–35 minutes, until tender. Drain well and leave to cool slightly.

2. Meanwhile, to make the pesto, put the parsley, capers and garlic into a mortar with the oil, walnuts, and salt and pepper to taste. Pound to a coarse paste using a pestle. Add the cheese and stir well.

3. When the potatoes are just cool enough to handle, peel off the skins and pass the flesh through a sieve into a large bowl or press through a potato ricer. While still hot, season well with salt and pepper and add the cheese.

4. Beat in the egg and sift in the flour. Lightly mix together, then turn out onto a lightly floured work surface. Lightly knead until the mixture becomes a smooth dough. If it is too sticky, add a little more flour.

5. Using your hands, roll out the dough on a lightly floured work surface into a long log.

6. Cut the log into 2.5-cm/1-inch pieces and gently press each piece with a fork to give the traditional ridged effect of gnocchi. Transfer the pieces to a floured baking sheet and cover with a clean tea towel.

SPECIAL OCCASIONS

7 Bring a large saucepan of water to the boil, add the gnocchi, in small batches, and cook for 1–2 minutes.

8 Remove with a slotted spoon and transfer to a warmed dish to keep warm while you cook the remaining gnocchi. Serve the gnocchi on warmed plates, topped with a good spoonful of the pesto.

SPROUTING BROCCOLI WITH CAPER BUTTER SAUCE

Serves: 4   **Prep: 25 mins**   **Cook: 20 mins**

Ingredients

700 g/1 lb 9 oz purple sprouting broccoli

3 tbsp extra virgin olive oil

3 shallots, thinly sliced

2 large garlic cloves, thinly sliced

pinch of red chilli flakes

3 tbsp pine nuts toasted

55 g/2 oz butter

2 tbsp capers, drained

4 tbsp snipped chives

25 g/1 oz vegetarian Parmesan-style cheese, shaved into wafers

sea salt and pepper

cooked pasta shapes, to serve

Method

1 Cut off the broccoli florets and slice lengthways if thick. Slice the leaves and stems into 2-cm/¾-inch pieces. Steam for 2 minutes over a saucepan of boiling water, until barely soft. Remove from the heat. Reserve the cooking water.

2 Heat the oil in a large frying pan over a medium–low heat. Add the shallots and fry for 5 minutes Add the garlic and fry for 2–3 minutes, until just starting to colour.

3 Increase the heat to medium and add the broccoli. Add the chilli flakes and season with salt and pepper. Add 3–4 tablespoons of the broccoli cooking water. Cook, stirring, for 4–6 minutes, until the broccoli is just tender and still bright green.

4 Stir in the pine nuts and check the seasoning. Tip into a serving dish and keep warm. Heat a heavy-based frying pan. When it is very hot, add the butter. Sizzle until golden. Remove from the heat and stir in the capers and half the chives.

5 Pour the sauce over the broccoli. Sprinkle with the cheese and the remaining chives. Serve immediately with the pasta.

PUMPKIN & CHESTNUT RISOTTO

Serves: 4 **Prep: 20 mins** **Cook: 35–40 mins**

Ingredients

1 tbsp olive oil

40 g/1½ oz butter

1 small onion, finely chopped

225 g/8 oz pumpkin, diced

225 g/8 oz chestnuts, cooked and shelled

280 g/10 oz risotto rice

150 ml/5 fl oz vegetarian dry white wine

1 tsp crumbled saffron threads (optional), dissolved in 4 tbsp of the stock

1 litre/1¾ pints simmering vegetable stock

85 g/3 oz vegetarian Parmesan-style cheese, freshly grated, plus extra for serving

salt and pepper

Method

1 Heat the oil with 25 g/1 oz of the butter in a deep saucepan over a medium heat until the butter has melted. Stir in the onion and pumpkin and cook, stirring occasionally, for 5 minutes, or until the onion is soft and starting to turn golden and the pumpkin begins to colour.

2 Roughly chop the chestnuts and add to the mixture. Stir thoroughly to coat.

3 Reduce the heat, add the rice and mix to coat in oil and butter. Cook, stirring constantly, for 2–3 minutes, or until the grains are translucent. Add the wine and cook, stirring constantly, for 1 minute, until it has reduced.

4 Add the saffron liquid to the rice, if using, and cook, stirring constantly, until the liquid has been absorbed.

5 Gradually add the simmering stock, a ladleful at a time, stirring constantly. Add more liquid as the rice absorbs each addition. Increase the heat to medium so that the liquid bubbles. Cook for 20 minutes, or until all the liquid has been absorbed and the rice is creamy. Season to taste with salt and pepper.

6 Remove from the heat and add the remaining butter and the cheese, stirring until melted. Serve immediately, sprinkled with extra cheese.

SPECIAL OCCASIONS

TOMATO SOUFFLÉ

Serves: 4

Prep: 20–25 mins, plus cooling

Cook: 1 hour– 1 hour 10 mins

Ingredients

350 g/12 oz potatoes, cut into chunks

plain flour, for dusting

1 beef tomato, peeled, deseeded and diced

1 egg, separated

1 tbsp olive oil, plus extra for brushing

4 egg whites

salt and pepper

Tomato sauce

25 g/1 oz butter

2 tbsp olive oil

1 onion, finely chopped

2 garlic cloves, finely chopped

1 celery stick, finely chopped

400 g/14 oz canned chopped tomatoes

2 tbsp tomato purée

brown sugar, to taste

1 tsp chopped fresh ginger

1 bay leaf

100 ml/3½ fl oz water

salt and pepper

Method

1 First, make the sauce. Melt the butter with the oil in a saucepan. Add the onion, garlic and celery and cook over a low heat, stirring occasionally, for 5 minutes, until softened. Stir in the canned tomatoes, tomato purée, sugar to taste, ginger, bay leaf and water and season to taste with salt and pepper. Increase the heat to medium and bring to the boil, then reduce the heat and simmer, stirring occasionally, for 15–20 minutes, until thickened.

2 Meanwhile, cook the potatoes in a large saucepan of salted boiling water for 20–25 minutes, until tender but not falling apart. Drain well and set aside.

3 Preheat the oven to 230°C/450°F/Gas Mark 8. Brush a 1.5-litre/2¾-pint soufflé dish with oil and dust with flour, tipping out the excess. Remove the sauce from the heat and leave to cool slightly. Remove and discard the bay leaf. Pour the sauce into a food processor, add the potatoes and process to a purée. Transfer to a bowl and stir in the diced tomato, egg yolk and oil. Taste and adjust the seasoning, adding salt and pepper if needed.

SPECIAL OCCASIONS

4 Whisk the egg whites in a grease-free bowl until they form soft peaks. Stir one quarter of the egg whites into the tomato mixture, then fold in the remainder. Pour into the prepared dish and bake in the preheated oven for 35–40 minutes, until risen and golden brown. Serve immediately.

RED CABBAGE STUFFED WITH MUSHROOMS, NUTS & RICE

Serves: 4-6   **Prep: 25-30 mins**   **Cook: 1 hour 25 mins–1½ hours**

Ingredients

50 g/1¾ oz butter, plus extra for greasing

1 large red cabbage

juice of 2 lemons

3 tbsp olive oil

1 onion, chopped

150 g/5½ oz mushrooms, chopped

175 g/6 oz mixed nuts, chopped

3 garlic cloves, chopped

2 tbsp chopped fresh oregano

115 g/4 oz cooked Camargue red rice

300 ml/10 fl oz vegetable stock

sea salt and pepper

Tomato Sauce

8-10 tomatoes

1 onion, sliced into thick rings

3 garlic cloves

2 tbsp groundnut oil

Method

1 Preheat the oven to 180°C/350°F/Gas Mark 4. Grease a 1-litre/1¾-pint round ovenproof dish with butter.

2 Bring a saucepan of lightly salted water to the boil. Remove 8–10 cabbage leaves and plunge into the boiling water. Add half the lemon juice and boil for 4 minutes. Drain and pat dry. Shave off the thickest part of the stalk.

3 Cut the remaining cabbage in half lengthways, reserving half for another recipe. Cut into quarters and discard the core. Shred the leaves.

4 Heat the oil and half the butter in a large frying pan over a medium heat. Add the onion and fry for 5 minutes, until translucent.

5 Add the mushrooms, nuts, shredded cabbage, garlic, oregano, and salt and pepper to taste and cook for 5 minutes.

6 Stir in the rice, remaining lemon juice and half the stock and cook for a further 2 minutes.

7 Arrange the cabbage leaves around the edge and base of the prepared dish, leaving no gaps. Fill with the stuffing, pressing it in well. Dot with the remaining butter.

8 Fold over the tops of the leaves. Pour the remaining stock round the edge. Tightly cover with thick foil, and bake in the preheated oven for 45–50 minutes.

9 To make the tomato sauce, place the tomatoes, onion and garlic under the hot grill and cook until blackened. Remove the tomato stalks but not the skins. Transfer to a food processor and process to a chunky purée. Heat the 2 tablespoons of oil in a frying pan. Stir in the tomato mixture and simmer for 10 minutes, until thickened. Season with salt and pepper, then pour into a large bowl. Serve the cabbage in wedges, accompanied by the tomato sauce.

KALE & BUTTER BEAN CASSEROLE

Serves: 6

Prep: 25 mins,
plus overnight soaking

Cook: 1¾–2 hours

Ingredients

350 g/12 oz butter beans, soaked overnight

1 tbsp cumin seeds

2 tsp dried oregano

3 tbsp groundnut oil

2 onions, chopped

2 garlic cloves, thinly sliced

1–3 fresh red or green chillies, deseeded and sliced

400 g/14 oz canned chopped tomatoes

450 ml/16 fl oz vegetable stock

175 g/6 oz shredded kale

5 tbsp chopped fresh coriander

juice of 1 lime

sea salt and pepper

2 avocados, cubed and tossed with lime juice, and red onion slivers, to garnish

Method

1 Drain the beans, put them into a large saucepan and cover with water. Boil rapidly for 15 minutes, then reduce the heat and simmer for 30–45 minutes, until tender but not disintegrating. Drain and set aside.

2 Put the cumin seeds into a small dry frying pan over a medium heat and fry until fragrant. Add the oregano, fry for a few seconds, then immediately remove the mixture from the pan Lightly crush the mixture in a mortar with a pestle.

3 Heat the oil in a large, flameproof casserole over a medium heat. Add the onions and the spice and herb mixture. Fry for 5 minutes, until the chopped onions are translucent. Add the garlic and chillies and fry for a further 2 minutes.

4 Stir in the tomatoes, beans and stock. Season with salt and pepper and bring to the boil. Reduce the heat, cover and simmer for 30 minutes, stirring occasionally. Increase the heat and stir in the kale. Simmer, uncovered,

for 7 minutes, or until tender but still brightly coloured. Stir in the coriander and lime juice. Ladle into soup plates, garnish with the avocado and red onion and serve immediately.

CARAMELIZED ONION TART

Serves: 4-6 **Prep: 20 mins** **Cook: 45-50 mins, plus resting**

Ingredients

100 g/3½ oz unsalted butter

600 g/1 lb 5 oz onions, thinly sliced

2 eggs

100 ml/3½ fl oz double cream

100 g/3½ oz vegetarian Gruyère cheese, grated

20-cm/8-inch ready-baked pastry case

100 g/3½ oz coarsely grated vegetarian Parmesan-style cheese

salt and pepper

Method

1 Melt the butter in a heavy-based frying pan over a medium heat. Add the onions and cook, stirring frequently to avoid burning, for 30 minutes, or until well-browned and caramelized. Remove the onions from the pan and set aside.

2 Preheat the oven to 190°C/375°F/Gas Mark 5. Beat the eggs in a large bowl. Stir in the cream and season to taste with salt and pepper. Add the Gruyère cheese and mix well. Stir in the cooked onions.

3 Pour the egg and onion mixture into the baked pastry case and sprinkle with the Parmesan-style cheese.

4 Place on a baking sheet and bake in the preheated oven for 15–20 minutes, until the filling has set and is beginning to brown. Remove from the oven and leave to rest for at least 10 minutes.

5 Cut the tart into slices and serve hot or at room temperature.

SPECIAL OCCASIONS

COURGETTE & BASIL RISOTTO

Serves: 4 **Prep: 20 mins** **Cook: 35–40 mins**

Ingredients

1.5 litres/2¾ pints vegetable stock

4 tbsp basil-flavoured extra virgin olive oil, plus extra for drizzling

4 courgettes, diced

1 yellow pepper, deseeded and diced

2 garlic cloves, finely chopped

1 large onion, finely chopped

400 g/14 oz risotto rice

4 tbsp dry white vermouth

2 tbsp unsalted butter

large handful of fresh basil leaves, torn, plus extra to garnish

85 g/3 oz vegetarian Parmesan-style cheese, grated

salt and pepper

Method

1 Bring the stock to the boil, then reduce the heat and keep simmering gently over a low heat while you are cooking the risotto.

2 Heat half the oil in a large frying pan over a high heat. When very hot, but not smoking, add the courgettes and yellow pepper and stir-fry for 3 minutes, until lightly golden. Stir in the garlic and cook for a further 30 seconds. Transfer to a plate and set aside.

3 Heat the remaining oil in a deep saucepan over a medium heat. Add the onion and cook, stirring occasionally, for about 2 minutes, until soft. Add the rice and cook, stirring frequently, for about 2 minutes, until the rice is translucent and well coated with the oil. Pour in the vermouth; it will bubble and steam rapidly and evaporate almost immediately.

4 Gradually add the hot stock, a ladleful at a time, stirring constantly. Add more stock as the rice absorbs each addition. Increase the heat so the liquid bubbles. Cook for 20–25 minutes, or until all the liquid has been absorbed and the rice is creamy but still firm to the bite.

5 Stir in the courgette mixture with any juices, the butter, basil and the cheese. Season to taste with salt and pepper. Drizzle with a little oil and garnish with basil. Serve immediately.

SPECIAL OCCASIONS

ROAST BEETROOT PARCELS WITH HORSERADISH BUTTER

Serves: 4

Prep: 25 mins,
plus cooling & chilling

Cook: 1¾ hours– 1 hour 55 mins

Ingredients

8 small beetroots, peeled and halved

olive oil, for greasing and tossing

4 fresh thyme sprigs

4 tbsp grated fresh horseradish, or grated horseradish from a jar

125 g/4½ oz unsalted butter

sea salt flakes and pepper

rocket leaves, to serve

Polenta

850 ml/1½ pints water

175 g/6 oz quick-cook polenta

1 tsp salt

Method

1 To make the polenta, bring the water to the boil in a large saucepan. Slowly add the polenta and salt, stirring constantly. Simmer, stirring frequently, for 30–40 minutes, until the mixture comes away from the side of the pan. Grease a small roasting tin. Tip the polenta into the tin, level the surface and leave to cool.

2 Preheat the oven to 190°C/375°F/Gas Mark 5. Toss the beetroots with enough oil to coat. Place 4 beetroot halves and a thyme sprig on a square of thick foil. Season to taste. Wrap in a loose parcel, sealing the edges. Repeat with the remaining beetroots. Roast in the preheated oven for about 1 hour or until just tender.

3 Meanwhile, mash the horseradish with the butter, ½ teaspoon of salt and ¼ teaspoon of pepper. Roll into a log using a piece of clingfilm and chill in the refrigerator.

4 Preheat the grill to high. Slice the polenta into four neat rectangles. Spread out in a grill pan, brush with oil and cook under a hot grill for 5 minutes. Turn and grill for a further 3 minutes, until crisp.

SPECIAL OCCASIONS

5 Unwrap the beetroot and horseradish butter. Arrange the polenta on serving plates. Place the beetroot and a slice of horseradish butter on top. Add a handful of rocket to each plate and serve immediately.

TOFU MOUSSAKA

Serves: 4

Prep: 30–35 mins, plus cooling

Cook: 1 hour 35 mins– 1 hour 40 mins

Ingredients

150 g/5½ oz baking potatoes, scrubbed

4 tbsp lemon juice

1 tsp rapeseed or vegetable oil

1 tsp sugar

2 tsp crushed garlic

1 tsp ground cumin

2 tbsp dried oregano

250 g/9 oz aubergine, diced

100 g/3½ oz onion, sliced

175 g/6 oz mixed peppers, deseeded and diced

200 g/7 oz canned chopped tomatoes

400 g/14 oz natural yogurt

2 tbsp cornflour

2 tbsp English mustard powder

200 g/7 oz silken tofu (drained weight), sliced

85 g/3 oz beef tomato, thinly sliced

pepper

Method

1 Preheat the oven to 190°C/375°F/Gas Mark 5. Bake the potatoes in their skins in the oven for 45 minutes, then remove and leave to cool. Cut into thin slices.

2 Mix the lemon juice, oil, sugar, garlic, cumin and oregano together in a small bowl, then lightly brush over the diced aubergine, reserving the remaining mixture. Spread out on a baking sheet and bake in the preheated oven for 15 minutes. Leave the oven on.

3 Heat the reserved lemon juice mixture in a frying pan over a high heat, add the onion and peppers and cook, stirring occasionally, until lightly browned. Add the canned tomatoes, reduce the heat and simmer for 4 minutes.

4 In a separate saucepan, whisk the yogurt and cornflour together, then bring to the boil, whisking constantly (to prevent the yogurt separating) until the yogurt boils and thickens. When the yogurt has thickened, remove from the heat and whisk in the mustard powder.

5 In an ovenproof dish, make layers of the potatoes, aubergine, onion and pepper mixture and tofu, adding yogurt sauce between each layer. Finish with a layer of beef tomato and top with the remaining yogurt sauce.

6 Bake in the preheated oven for 20–25 minutes, or until golden brown on top. Season with pepper and serve immediately.

VEGETARIAN PAELLA

Serves: 6   **Prep: 20 mins**   **Cook: 40 mins**

Ingredients

½ tsp saffron threads

2 tbsp hot water

6 tbsp olive oil

1 Spanish onion, sliced

3 garlic cloves, crushed

1 red pepper, deseeded and sliced

1 orange pepper, deseeded and sliced

1 large aubergine, cubed

200 g/7 oz paella rice

600 ml/1 pint vegetable stock

450 g/1 lb tomatoes, peeled and chopped

115 g/4 oz button mushrooms, sliced

115 g/4 oz French beans, halved

400 g/14 oz canned pinto beans

salt and pepper

Method

1 Put the saffron threads and water in a small bowl and leave to infuse for a few minutes.

2 Meanwhile, heat the oil in a paella pan or wide, shallow frying pan and cook the onion over a medium heat, stirring, for 2–3 minutes, or until softened. Add the garlic, peppers and aubergine and cook, stirring frequently, for 5 minutes.

3 Add the rice and cook, stirring constantly, for 1 minute, or until glossy and coated in oil. Pour in the stock and add the tomatoes, saffron and its soaking water, and salt and pepper to taste. Bring to the boil, then reduce the heat and simmer, shaking the pan frequently and stirring occasionally, for 15 minutes.

4 Stir in the mushrooms, French beans and pinto beans with their can juices. Cook for a further 10 minutes, then serve immediately.

SQUASH, KALE & FARRO STEW

Serves: 6　　　　**Prep: 20–25 mins**　　　**Cook: 1 hour**

Ingredients

1 dense-fleshed squash, such as Kabocha or Crown Prince, weighing about 1.25 kg/2 lb 12 oz

2 tbsp vegetable oil

1 onion, finely chopped

2 tsp dried oregano

2 garlic cloves, finely sliced

400 g/14 oz canned chopped tomatoes

700 ml/1¼ pints vegetable stock

125 g/4½ oz quick-cook farro, rinsed

250 g/9 oz kale, sliced into ribbons

400 g/14 oz canned chickpeas, drained and rinsed

6 tbsp chopped fresh coriander

juice of 1 lime

salt and pepper

Method

1 Cut the squash into quarters, peel and deseed. Cut the flesh into large cubes (you will need about 650 g/1 lb 7 oz).

2 Heat the oil in a flameproof casserole or heavy-based saucepan. Add the onion and fry over a medium heat for 5 minutes, until translucent. Add the oregano and garlic and fry for 2 minutes.

3 Add the squash and cook, covered, for 10 minutes.

4 Add the tomatoes, stock and farro, cover and bring to the boil. Reduce the heat to a gentle simmer and cook for 20 minutes, stirring occasionally.

5 Add the kale and chickpeas. Cook for a further 15 minutes, or until the kale is just tender.

6 Season to taste with salt and pepper. Stir in the coriander and lime juice just before serving.

★ **Variation**

Use 400 g/14 oz canned drained borlotti beans instead of the chickpeas.

DESSERTS

RICE PUDDING 208

LATTICED CHERRY PIE 210

CHOCOLATE MOUSSE 212

STRAWBERRY CHEESECAKE 214

ETON MESS 216

PEACH COBBLER 218

FIG & WATERMELON SALAD 219

KEY LIME PIE 220

SALTED CARAMEL PIES 222

LEMON MERINGUE PIE 224

NEW YORK CHEESECAKE 226

RICH CHOCOLATE TARTS 228

RED WINE SORBET 229

APPLE & BLACKBERRY CRUMBLE 230

CRÈME BRÛLÉE 231

RASPBERRY & WHITE CHOCOLATE BRÛLÉES 232

SUMMER PAVLOVA 234

ICE-CREAM BROWNIE SUNDAE 236

TOFFEE CHOCOLATE PUFF TARTS 238

CAPPUCCINO SOUFFLÉS 240

STICKY COFFEE & WALNUT SPONGES 242

FRESH BLACK CHERRY PIES 244

FRUIT COCKTAIL POPS 246

CHOCOLATE ICE-CREAM BITES 247

SWEET PUMPKIN PIE 248

BANANA CREAM PIE 250

MANGO & PASSION FRUIT FOOL 252

RICE PUDDING

Serves: 4–6   **Prep: 15 mins**   **Cook: 1 hour 35 mins–
2 hours 5 mins**

Ingredients

115 g/4 oz pudding rice

55 g/2 oz caster sugar

850 ml/1½ pints milk

½ tsp vanilla extract

40 g/1½ oz unsalted butter,
chilled, plus extra
for greasing

whole nutmeg, for grating

Method

1 Preheat the oven to 150°C/300°F/Gas Mark 2.
Grease a 1.2-litre/2-pint baking dish. Place the
rice in the dish and sprinkle with the sugar.

2 Heat the milk in a saucepan until almost boiling,
then pour over the rice. Add the vanilla extract
and stir well to dissolve the sugar.

3 Cut the butter into small pieces and scatter over
the surface of the pudding.

4 Grate nutmeg to taste over the top. Place the
dish on a baking sheet and bake in the centre
of the preheated oven for 1½–2 hours, or until
the pudding is well browned on the top. Stir after
the first 30 minutes of cooking to disperse the
rice. Serve hot, topped with one or more of the
accompaniments, if using.

★ Variation

Top the rice pudding with either cream, jam,
fresh fruit purée, stewed fruit, honey or ice cream.

LATTICED CHERRY PIE

Serves: 8

Prep: 35 mins,
plus chilling

Cook: 55-60 mins

Ingredients

Pastry

140 g/5 oz plain flour,
plus extra for dusting

¼ tsp baking powder

½ tsp mixed spice

½ tsp salt

50 g/1¾ oz caster sugar

55 g/2 oz unsalted butter,
chilled and diced,
plus extra for greasing

1 egg, beaten, plus extra
for glazing

Filling

900 g/2 lb stoned fresh
cherries, or canned cherries,
drained

150 g/5½ oz caster sugar

½ tsp almond extract

2 tsp cherry brandy

¼ tsp mixed spice

2 tbsp cornflour

2 tbsp water

25 g/1 oz unsalted butter,
melted

ice cream, to serve

Method

1 To make the pastry, sift the flour with the baking powder into a large bowl. Stir in the mixed spice, salt and sugar. Rub the butter until the mixture resembles fine breadcrumbs, make a well in the centre, pour in the egg and mix into a dough.

2 Cut the dough in half, and use your hands to roll each half into a ball. Wrap and chill for 30 minutes. Preheat the oven to 220°C/425°F/ Gas Mark 7.

3 Grease a 23-cm/9-inch round pie dish. Roll out the doughs into two rounds, each 30 cm/12 inches in diameter. Use one to line the pie dish.

4 To make the filling, put half the cherries and all the sugar in a saucepan. Bring to a simmer and stir in the almond extract, brandy and mixed spice. In a bowl, mix the cornflour and water into a paste. Stir the paste into the saucepan, then boil until the mixture thickens. Stir in the remaining cherries, pour into the pastry case, then dot with butter.

5 Cut the remaining pastry into strips 1 cm/½ inch wide. Lay the strips over the filling, crossing to form a lattice. Trim and seal the edges with water. Use your fingers to crimp around the rim, then glaze the top with the beaten egg. Cover with kitchen foil, then bake for 30 minutes in the preheated oven. Remove from the oven, discard the foil, then bake for a further 15 minutes, or until golden. Serve with ice cream.

CHOCOLATE MOUSSE

Serves: 4–6

Prep: 35 mins,
plus cooling & chilling

Cook: 5 mins

Ingredients

225 g/8 oz plain chocolate, chopped

2 tbsp brandy, Grand Marnier or Cointreau

4 tbsp water

25 g/1 oz unsalted butter, diced

3 large eggs, separated

¼ tsp cream of tartar

55 g/2 oz sugar

125 ml/4 fl oz double cream

Method

1 Place the chocolate, brandy and water in a small saucepan over low heat and melt, stirring, until smooth. Remove the pan from the heat and beat in the butter. Beat the egg yolks into the chocolate mixture, one after another, until blended, then cool slightly.

2 Meanwhile, using an electric mixer on low speed, beat the egg whites in a spotlessly clean bowl until frothy, then gradually increase the mixer's speed and beat until soft peaks form. Sprinkle the cream of tartar over the surface, then add the sugar, tablespoon by tablespoon, and continue beating until stiff peaks form. Beat several tablespoons of the egg whites into the chocolate mixture to loosen.

3 In another bowl, whip the cream until soft peaks form. Spoon the cream over the chocolate mixture, then spoon the remaining whites over the cream. Use a large spoon or spatula to fold the chocolate into the cream and egg whites. Either spoon the chocolate mousse into a large serving bowl or divide between individual bowls. Cover the bowls with clingfilm and chill the mousse for at least 3 hours before serving.

DESSERTS

STRAWBERRY CHEESECAKE

Serves: 8

Prep: 25 mins,
plus cooling

Cook: 1 hour 10 mins,
plus cooling in turned off oven

Ingredients

Base

55 g/2 oz unsalted butter

200 g/7 oz digestive biscuits, crushed

85 g/3 oz chopped walnuts

Filling

450 g/1 lb vegetarian mascarpone cheese

2 eggs, beaten

3 tbsp caster sugar

250 g/9 oz white chocolate, broken into pieces

300 g/10½ oz strawberries, hulled and quartered

Topping

175 g/6 oz vegetarian mascarpone cheese

50 g/1¾ oz white chocolate shavings

4 strawberries, halved

Method

1 Preheat the oven to 150°C/300°F/Gas Mark 2. Melt the butter in a saucepan over a low heat and stir in the crushed biscuits and walnuts.

2 Spoon into a 23-cm/9-inch springform cake tin and press evenly over the base with the back of a spoon. Set aside.

3 To make the filling, beat the mascarpone cheese in a bowl until smooth, then beat in the eggs and sugar.

4 Melt the white chocolate in a heatproof bowl set over a saucepan of gently simmering water, stirring until smooth. Remove from the heat and leave to cool slightly, then stir into the cheese mixture. Stir in the strawberries.

5 Spoon the mixture into the cake tin, spread evenly and smooth the surface. Bake in the preheated oven for 1 hour, or until just firm.

6 Turn off the oven and leave the cheesecake inside with the door slightly ajar until completely cold. Transfer to a serving plate.

7 Spread the mascarpone cheese on top, decorate with the chocolate shavings and the strawberry halves and serve.

ETON MESS

Serves: 4–6

Prep: 35–40 mins, plus cooling

Cook: 45–50 mins

Ingredients

3 egg whites

175 g/6 oz caster sugar

700 g/1 lb 9 oz strawberries

2 tbsp icing sugar

2 tbsp crème de fraise (strawberry) liqueur (optional)

300 ml/10 fl oz double cream

150 ml/5 fl oz single cream

Method

1 Preheat the oven to 150°C/300°F/Gas Mark 2. Whisk the egg whites in a clean bowl using an electric mixer until thick and in soft peaks. Add the sugar gradually, whisking well after each addition. The meringue mixture should be glossy and firm. Spoon the meringue onto a baking sheet lined with baking paper and spread into a rough 30-cm/12-inch round. Cook in the preheated oven for 45–50 minutes until the meringue is firm on the outside but still soft in the centre. Remove from the oven and allow to cool.

2 Check over the strawberries and hull them. Place a third of the strawberries (choose the larger ones) in a liquidizer and purée with the icing sugar. Pour the purée into a bowl, add the liqueur, if using, and the remaining strawberries and turn in the sauce until well mixed. Whip together the double and single cream until thick but still light and floppy.

3 Break the meringue into large pieces and place half in a large glass serving bowl. Spoon over half the fruit mixture and half the cream. Layer up the remaining ingredients and lightly fold the mixtures together so you have a streaky appearance. Serve immediately after mixing or the meringues will soften.

DESSERTS

PEACH COBBLER

Serves: 4–6   **Prep: 20–30 mins**   **Cook: 35 mins**

Ingredients

Filling

6 peaches, peeled and sliced

4 tbsp caster sugar

½ tbsp lemon juice

1½ tsp cornflour

½ tsp almond or
vanilla extract

vanilla or pecan ice cream,
to serve

Topping

185 g/6½ oz plain flour

115 g/4 oz caster sugar

1½ tsp baking powder

½ tsp salt

85 g/3 oz butter, diced

1 egg

6 tbsp milk

Method

1 Preheat the oven to 220°C/425°F/Gas Mark 7.
Place the peaches in a 23-cm/9-inch square
baking dish. Add the sugar, lemon juice, cornflour
and almond extract and toss together. Bake in
the preheated oven for 20 minutes.

2 Meanwhile, to make the topping, sift the flour,
all but 2 tablespoons of the sugar, the baking
powder and the salt into a bowl. Rub in the
butter with the fingertips until the mixture
resembles breadcrumbs. Mix the egg and
5 tablespoons of the milk in a jug, then mix into
the dry ingredients with a fork until a soft, sticky
dough forms. If the dough seems too dry, stir in
the extra tablespoon of milk.

3 Reduce the oven temperature to 200°C/400°F/
Gas Mark 6. Remove the peaches from the
oven and drop spoonfuls of the topping over
the surface, without smoothing. Sprinkle with the
remaining sugar, return to the oven and bake
for a further 15 minutes, or until the topping is
golden brown and firm – the topping will spread
as it cooks. Serve hot or at room temperature,
with ice cream.

DESSERTS

FIG & WATERMELON SALAD

Serves: 4

Prep: 20–25 mins,
plus cooling & chilling

Cook: 5 mins

Ingredients

1.5 kg/3 lb 5 oz watermelon

115 g/4 oz seedless
black grapes

4 figs

Syrup dressing

1 lime

grated rind and juice of
1 orange

1 tbsp maple syrup

2 tbsp honey

Method

1 Cut the watermelon into wedges and scoop out
and discard the seeds. Cut the flesh away from
the rind, then chop the flesh into 2.5-cm/1-inch
cubes. Put the watermelon cubes in a bowl with
the grapes. Cut each fig lengthways into eight
wedges and add to the bowl.

2 Grate the lime and mix the rind with the orange
rind and juice, maple syrup and honey in a small
saucepan. Bring to the boil over a low heat. Pour
the mixture over the fruit and stir. Leave to cool.
Stir again, cover and chill in the refrigerator for at
least 1 hour, stirring occasionally.

3 Divide the fruit salad equally between four
bowls to serve.

DESSERTS

KEY LIME PIE

Serves: 8

Prep: 25–30 mins, plus cooling & chilling

Cook: 25 mins

Ingredients

Biscuit crust

175 g/6 oz digestive or ginger biscuits

2 tbsp caster sugar

½ tsp ground cinnamon

70 g/2½ oz butter, melted, plus extra for greasing

Filling

400 g/14 oz canned condensed milk

125 ml/4 fl oz freshly squeezed lime juice

finely grated rind of 3 limes

4 egg yolks

whipped cream, to serve

Method

1 Preheat the oven to 160°C/325°F/Gas Mark 3. Grease a 23-cm/9-inch round tart tin, about 4 cm/1½ inches deep.

2 To make the biscuit crust, put the biscuits, sugar and cinnamon in a food processor and process until fine crumbs form – do not overprocess to a powder. Add the melted butter and process again until moistened.

3 Tip the crumb mixture into the prepared tart tin and press evenly into the base and sides. Place the tart tin on a baking sheet and bake in the preheated oven for 5 minutes. Meanwhile, beat the condensed milk, lime juice, lime rind and egg yolks together in a bowl until well blended.

4 Remove the tart tin from the oven, pour the filling into the biscuit crust and spread out to the edges. Return to the oven for a further 15 minutes, or until the filling is set around the edges but still wobbly in the centre. Leave to cool completely on a wire rack, then cover and chill for at least 2 hours. Serve spread thickly with whipped cream.

SALTED CARAMEL PIES

Makes: 4

Prep: 30 mins,
plus chilling & cooling

Cook: 15 mins

Ingredients

Crumb crust

175 g/6 oz digestive biscuits,
finely crushed

85 g/3 oz butter, melted

Filling

300 g/10½ oz caster sugar

150 g/5½ oz butter

¼ tsp sea salt crystals

125 ml/4 fl oz double cream

Topping

150 ml/5 fl oz double cream

chocolate curls or shavings

Method

1 To make the crumb crust, place the crushed biscuits in a bowl and stir in the melted butter. Divide the mixture between four tartlet tins and press down firmly into the base and up the sides of each tin. Chill in the refrigerator for 30 minutes.

2 To make the filling, place the sugar and 4 tablespoons of water into a heavy-based saucepan. Heat gently, stirring, until the sugar has dissolved. Bring the syrup to a boil and boil, without stirring, until the liquid is a golden toffee colour. Remove from the heat and cool for 2 minutes, then carefully stir in the butter and half the salt.

3 Gradually whisk in the cream and continue whisking until the mixture is smooth and glossy. Transfer to a heatproof bowl and leave to cool and thicken, stirring occasionally. Stir in the rest of the salt. Spoon the cooled caramel into the tartlet cases.

4 For the topping, whip the cream until holding soft peaks. Drop large spoonfuls on top of the caramel filling, scatter over the chocolate curls or shavings and serve.

DESSERTS

LEMON MERINGUE PIE

Serves: 6–8

Prep: 40 mins,
plus chilling & cooling

Cook: 1 hour

Ingredients

Pastry

150 g/5½ oz plain flour, plus extra for dusting

85 g/3 oz butter, cut into small pieces, plus extra for greasing

35 g/1¼ oz icing sugar, sifted

finely grated rind of ½ lemon

½ egg yolk, beaten

1½ tbsp milk

Filling

3 tbsp cornflour

300 ml/10 fl oz water

juice and grated rind of 2 lemons

175 g/6 oz caster sugar

2 eggs, separated

Method

1 To make the pastry, sift the flour into a bowl. Rub in the butter with your fingertips until the mixture resembles fine breadcrumbs.

2 Mix in the remaining pastry ingredients. Turn out onto a lightly floured work surface and knead briefly. Wrap in clingfilm and chill in the refrigerator for 30 minutes.

3 Preheat the oven to 180°C/350°F/Gas Mark 4. Grease a 20-cm/8-inch round tart tin. Roll out the pastry to a thickness of 5 mm/¼ inch, then use to line the tin.

4 Prick all over with a fork, line with baking paper and fill with baking beans. Bake blind in the preheated oven for 15 minutes.

5 Remove the pastry case from the oven and take out the paper and beans. Reduce the oven temperature to 150°C/300°F/Gas Mark 2.

6 To make the filling, mix the cornflour with a little of the water to form a paste. Put the remaining water in a saucepan. Stir in the lemon juice, lemon rind and cornflour paste.

7 Bring to the boil, stirring. Cook for 2 minutes. Leave to cool slightly. Stir in 5 tablespoons of the caster sugar and the egg yolks. Pour into the pastry case.

8 Whisk the egg whites until stiff. Gradually whisk in the remaining caster sugar and spread over the pie. Return to the oven and bake for a further 40 minutes.

9 Remove from the oven, leave to cool and serve.

NEW YORK CHEESECAKE

Serves: 10

Prep: 35 mins,
plus cooling & chilling

Cook: 1 hour,
plus cooling & setting

Ingredients

100 g/3½ oz butter,
plus extra for greasing

150 g/5½ oz digestive
biscuits, finely crushed

1 tbsp granulated sugar

900 g/2 lb cream cheese

250 g/9 oz caster sugar

2 tbsp plain flour

1 tsp vanilla extract

finely grated zest of
1 orange

finely grated zest of
1 lemon

3 eggs

2 egg yolks

300 ml/10 fl oz double
cream

Method

1 Preheat the oven to 180°C/350°F/Gas Mark 4.
Melt the butter in a small saucepan. Remove
from the heat and stir in the biscuits and sugar.

2 Press the biscuit mixture tightly into the base of
a 23-cm/9-inch springform round cake tin. Place
in the preheated oven and bake for 10 minutes.
Remove from the oven and leave to cool on a
wire rack.

3 Increase the oven temperature to 200°C/400°F/
Gas Mark 6. Use an electric mixer to beat the
cheese until creamy, then gradually add the
caster sugar and flour and beat until smooth.

4 Increase the speed and beat in the vanilla
extract, orange zest and lemon zest, then beat
in the eggs and egg yolks one at a time. Finally,
beat in the cream. Scrape any excess from the
sides and paddles of the beater into the mixture.
It should be light and fluffy – beat on a faster
setting if you need to.

5 Grease the sides of the cake tin and pour in the
filling. Smooth the top, transfer to the oven
and bake for 15 minutes, then reduce the
temperature to 110°C/225°F/Gas Mark ¼ and
bake for a further 30 minutes.

6 Turn off the oven and leave the cheesecake in it for 2 hours to cool and set. Chill in the refrigerator overnight before serving.

7 Slide a knife around the edge of the cake then unfasten the tin, cut the cheesecake into slices and serve.

RICH CHOCOLATE TARTS

Serves: 8

Prep: 35–40 mins,
plus chilling & cooling

Cook: 25–30 mins

Ingredients

225 g/8 oz plain flour,
plus extra for dusting

115 g/4 oz butter, diced

2 tbsp icing sugar

1 egg yolk

2–3 tbsp cold water

Filling

250 g/9 oz plain chocolate,
broken into pieces,
plus extra to decorate

115 g/4 oz butter

50 g/1¾ oz icing sugar

300 ml/10 fl oz double
cream

Method

1 Place the flour in a large bowl. Add the butter and rub it in with your fingertips until the mixture resembles breadcrumbs. Add the icing sugar, egg yolk and enough water to form a soft dough. Cover and chill for 15 minutes. Roll the pastry out on a lightly floured work surface and use to line 8 x 10-cm/4-inch shallow tartlet cases. Chill for 30 minutes.

2 Preheat the oven to 200°C/400°F/Gas Mark 6. Prick the base of the cases with a fork and line with a little crumpled foil. Bake in the preheated oven for 10 minutes, then remove the foil and bake for 5–10 minutes, until crisp. Transfer to a wire rack to cool. Reduce the oven temperature to 160°C/325°F/Gas Mark 3.

3 To make the filling, place the chocolate, butter and icing sugar in a heatproof bowl set over a saucepan of simmering water and heat until melted. Remove from the heat and stir in 200 ml/7 fl oz double cream. Remove the cases from the tins and place on a baking sheet. Fill each case with the chocolate. Bake for 5 minutes. Cool, then chill until required. To serve, whip the remaining cream and pipe or spoon into the centre of each tart. Grate the plain chocolate and use to decorate.

DESSERTS

RED WINE SORBET

Serves: 6

Prep: 30 mins,
plus cooling & freezing

Cook: 10 mins

Ingredients

1 orange

1 lemon

600 ml/1 pint vegetarian
fruity red wine

140 g/5 oz soft light
brown sugar

300 ml/10 fl oz water, chilled

2 egg whites, lightly beaten

fresh fruit, to serve

Method

1 Peel the zest from the orange and lemon in strips using a potato peeler, being careful not to remove any of the bitter white pith underneath. Place in a saucepan with the red wine and sugar. Heat gently, stirring until the sugar dissolves, then bring to the boil and simmer for 5 minutes. Remove from the heat and stir in the water.

2 Squeeze the juice from the fruit. Stir into the wine mixture. Cover and leave until completely cooled then strain into a freezerproof container. Cover and freeze for 7–8 hours, or until firm.

3 Working quickly, break the sorbet into chunks and transfer to a food processor. Blend for a few seconds to break down the chunks then, leaving the processor running, gradually pour the egg whites through the feed tube. The mixture will become paler. Continue blending until smooth.

4 Freeze for a further 3–4 hours, or until firm. Scoop into six chilled glasses or dishes and serve immediately with the fresh fruit.

DESSERTS

APPLE & BLACKBERRY CRUMBLE

Serves: 4　　　　**Prep: 20–25 mins**　　　　**Cook: 40–45 mins**

Ingredients

900 g/2 lb cooking apples

300 g/10½ oz blackberries, fresh or frozen

55 g/2 oz light muscovado sugar

1 tsp ground cinnamon

85 g/3 oz self-raising flour

85 g/3 oz wholemeal plain flour

115 g/4 oz unsalted butter, diced

55 g/2 oz demerara sugar

custard or pouring cream, to serve

Method

1　Preheat the oven to 200°C/400°F/Gas Mark 6. Peel and core the apples, then cut them into chunks. Put them in a bowl with the blackberries, muscovado sugar and cinnamon and mix together, then transfer to a baking dish.

2　To make the crumble topping, sieve the self-raising flour into a bowl and stir in the wholemeal flour. Rub in the butter with your fingertips until the mixture resembles coarse breadcrumbs. Stir in the demerara sugar.

3　Spread the crumble topping over the fruit and bake in the preheated oven for 40–45 minutes, or until the apples are soft and the crumble is golden brown and crisp. Serve with custard or pouring cream.

CRÈME BRÛLÉE

Serves: 6

Prep: 20–25 mins, plus chilling   **Cook: 2–4 mins**

Ingredients

225–300 g/8–10½ oz mixed soft fruits, such as blueberries and stoned fresh cherries

1½–2 tbsp orange liqueur or orange flower water

250 g/9 oz vegetarian mascarpone cheese

200 ml/7 fl oz crème fraîche

2–3 tbsp dark muscovado sugar

Method

1 Prepare the fruit, if necessary, and lightly rinse, then place in the bases of six 150-ml/5 fl oz ramekin dishes. Sprinkle the fruit with the liqueur.

2 Cream the mascarpone cheese in a bowl until soft, then gradually beat in the crème fraîche.

3 Spoon the cheese mixture over the fruit, smoothing the surface and ensuring that the tops are level. Chill in the refrigerator for at least 2 hours.

4 Sprinkle the tops with the sugar. Using a chef's blow torch, grill the tops until caramelized (about 2–3 minutes). Alternatively, cook under a preheated grill, turning the dishes, for 3–4 minutes, or until the tops are lightly caramelized all over.

5 Serve immediately or chill in the refrigerator for 15–20 minutes before serving.

DESSERTS

RASPBERRY & WHITE CHOCOLATE BRÛLÉES

Serves: 6

Prep: 20 mins,
plus cooling & chilling

Cook: 10 mins

Ingredients

200 g/7 oz white chocolate,
broken into pieces

200 ml/7 fl oz single cream

500 g/1 lb 2 oz Greek yogurt

225 g/8 oz raspberries

75 g/3 oz granulated sugar

3 tbsp water

Method

1 Place the chocolate and single cream in a heatproof bowl. Set the bowl over a saucepan of simmering water and heat, stirring occasionally until melted and smooth. Remove from the heat and leave to cool slightly.

2 Stir the chocolate mixture into the yogurt, then fold in the raspberries. Divide between six x 150 ml/5 fl oz ramekin dishes and level the surfaces with the back of a teaspoon. Chill in the refrigerator for at least 30 minutes.

3 Place the granulated sugar and water in a small heavy-based pan. Heat gently until the sugar dissolves, then turn up the heat and boil rapidly, for about 4 minutes, without stirring until the sugar turns a rich caramel colour.

4 Remove from the heat and let the bubbles subside, then quickly spoon some caramel over the top of each ramekin. The topping will set almost instantly. Serve immediately or chill and serve within 3 hours whilst the caramel is still crisp.

★ **Variation**

Try strawberries or blueberries instead of raspberries.

SUMMER PAVLOVA

Serves: 6

Prep: 30 mins, plus cooling

Cook: 1½–2 hours, plus cooling in turned off oven

Ingredients

Meringue
2 egg whites
40 g/1½ oz caster sugar
1 tsp cornflour
1 tsp vanilla extract
1 tsp vinegar

Filling
200 g/7 oz low-fat
cream cheese
150 g/5½ oz low-fat natural
yogurt
½–1 tsp vanilla extract,
or to taste
300 g/10½ oz mixed berries

Method

1 Preheat the oven to 120°C/250°F/Gas Mark ½ and line a baking sheet with baking paper. To make the meringue, whisk the egg whites in a large, greasefree bowl until stiff then gradually add the sugar a spoonful at a time, whisking well after each addition. Stir in the cornflour, vanilla extract and the vinegar.

2 When all the sugar has been added and the mixture is stiff, spoon onto the lined baking sheet and form into a 15-cm/6-inch round, hollowing out the centre to form a case.

3 Bake in the preheated oven for 1½–2 hours, or until crisp. Switch the oven off and leave to cool in the oven. Remove from the oven and leave until cold before removing from the baking sheet. Store in an airtight container until required.

4 To make the filling, beat the cream cheese and yogurt together in a bowl until well blended, then stir in the vanilla extract. Clean the fruits, if necessary, and cut any large fruits into bite-sized pieces. When ready to serve, pile the cheese filling in the centre of the pavlova case, top with the fruits and serve, cut into six pieces.

ICE-CREAM BROWNIE SUNDAE

Serves: 6

Prep: 30 mins,
plus cooling

Cook: 45–50 mins

Ingredients

175 g/6 oz plain chocolate, broken into pieces

175 g/6 oz butter, plus extra for greasing

175 g/6 oz soft light brown sugar

3 eggs, beaten

115 g/4 oz self-raising flour

Chocolate fudge sauce

55 g/2 oz plain chocolate, broken into pieces

55 g/2 oz light soft brown sugar

55 g/2 oz unsalted butter

3 tbsp milk

To serve

6 large scoops of vanilla ice cream

1 tbsp pecan nuts, chopped

6 fresh or maraschino cherries

Method

1 Preheat the oven to 180°C/350°F/Gas Mark 4. Grease a 20-cm/8-inch square cake tin and line with baking paper.

2 For the brownies, place the chocolate and butter in a large heatproof bowl set over a pan of simmering water and leave until melted. Cool for 5 minutes then whisk in the sugar and eggs. Sift over the flour and fold in. Pour the mixture into the prepared cake tin and bake in the preheated oven for 35–40 minutes, or until risen and just firm to the touch. Leave to cool in the tin for 15 minutes, then turn out onto a wire rack to cool completely.

3 For the sauce, place all the ingredients in a saucepan and heat gently, stirring all the time until melted. Bring to the boil and bubble for 1 minute. Remove from the heat and leave for 20 minutes.

4 To serve, cut the brownies into six pieces. Place each piece on a serving plate and top with a large scoop of ice cream. Spoon over the warm sauce and decorate with the chopped pecan nuts and cherries.

TOFFEE CHOCOLATE PUFF TARTS

Serves: 6

Prep: 40 mins,
plus chilling & cooling

Cook: 25–30 mins

Ingredients

375 g/13 oz ready-rolled puff pastry

140 g/5 oz plain chocolate, broken into pieces

300 ml/10 fl oz double cream

50 g/1¾ oz caster sugar

4 egg yolks

4 tbsp ready-made toffee sauce

whipped cream, to serve

cocoa powder, for dusting

Method

1 Line the bases of a 12-cup muffin tin with discs of baking paper. Cut out 12 x 5-cm/2-inch rounds from the edge of the pastry and cut the remainder into 12 strips. Roll the strips to half their thickness and line the sides of each hole with one strip. Place a disc of pastry in each base and press together to seal and make a tart case. Prick the bases and chill in the refrigerator for 30 minutes.

2 Preheat the oven to 200°C/400°F/Gas Mark 6. While the pastry is chilling, place the chocolate in a heatproof bowl, set the bowl over a saucepan of gently simmering water and heat until melted. Leave to cool slightly, then stir in the cream.

3 Place the sugar and egg yolks in a bowl and beat together, then mix well with the melted chocolate. Place a teaspoonful of the toffee sauce into each tart case, then divide the chocolate mixture evenly between the tarts.

4 Bake in the preheated oven for 20–25 minutes, turning the tin around halfway through cooking, until just set. Leave to cool in the tin, then remove carefully and serve with whipped cream, dusted with cocoa.

CAPPUCCINO SOUFFLÉS

Serves: 6 **Prep: 30 mins,** **Cook: 25 mins**
plus cooling

Ingredients

6 tbsp whipping cream

2 tsp instant espresso coffee granules

2 tbsp Kahlúa

butter, for greasing

3 large eggs, separated, plus 1 extra egg white

2 tbsp golden caster sugar, plus extra for coating

150 g/5½ oz plain chocolate, melted and cooled

cocoa powder, for dusting

Method

1 Place the cream in a small, heavy-based saucepan and heat gently. Stir in the coffee until it has dissolved, then stir in the Kahlúa. Divide the coffee mixture between six lightly greased 175-ml/6-fl oz ramekins coated with caster sugar. Preheat the oven to 190°C/375°F/Gas Mark 5.

2 Place the egg whites in a clean bowl and whisk until soft peaks form, then gradually whisk in the sugar until stiff but not dry. Stir the egg yolks and melted chocolate together in a separate bowl, then stir in a little of the whisked egg whites. Gradually fold in the remaining egg whites.

3 Divide the mixture between the prepared ramekins. Place the ramekins on a baking sheet and bake in the preheated oven for 15 minutes, or until just set. Dust with sifted cocoa powder and serve immediately.

STICKY COFFEE & WALNUT SPONGES

Serves: 6   **Prep: 35 mins**   **Cook: 30–40 mins**

Ingredients

1 tbsp instant coffee powder

150 g/5½ oz self-raising flour

1 tsp ground cinnamon

55 g/2 oz butter, softened, plus extra for greasing

55 g/2 oz brown sugar, sifted

2 large eggs, beaten

55 g/2 oz walnuts, finely chopped

Butterscotch sauce

25 g/1 oz walnuts, roughly chopped

55 g/2 oz butter

55 g/2 oz brown sugar

Method

1 Dissolve the coffee powder in 2 tablespoons of boiling water and set aside. Sift the flour and cinnamon into a bowl. Place the butter and sugar in a separate bowl and beat together until light and fluffy. Gradually beat in the eggs. Add a little of the flour mixture if the mixture shows signs of curdling. Fold in half the flour and cinnamon mixture, then fold in the remaining flour and cinnamon, alternately with the coffee and walnuts. Preheat the oven to 190°C/375°F/ Gas Mark 5.

2 Divide the mixture between six small, greased pudding basins. Place a piece of greased foil over each basin and secure with an elastic band. Stand the basins in a roasting tin and pour in enough boiling water to reach halfway up the sides of the basins. Cover the roasting tin with a tent of foil, folding it under the rim.

3 Bake in the preheated oven for 30–40 minutes, or until well risen and firm to the touch. Meanwhile, make the sauce. Place all the ingredients in a saucepan over low heat and stir until melted and blended. Bring to a simmer, then remove from the heat. Turn the sponges out on to a serving plate, spoon over the hot sauce and serve.

FRESH BLACK CHERRY PIES

Makes: 8

Prep: 40 mins,
plus chilling & cooling

Cook: 30–35 mins

Ingredients

Pastry

225 g/8 oz plain flour,
plus extra for dusting

115 g/4 oz butter, diced

2 tbsp icing sugar

1 tsp vanilla extract

1 egg yolk

2–3 tbsp cold water

Filling

250 g/9 oz vegetarian
mascarpone

55 g/2 oz icing sugar

2 eggs

150 ml/5 fl oz double cream

250 g/9 oz black cherries

3 tbsp black cherry or
blackcurrant jam

1 tbsp water

Method

1 Place the flour in a large bowl. Add the butter to the flour and rub it in with your fingertips until the mixture resembles fine breadcrumbs. Add the icing sugar, vanilla extract, egg yolk and enough water to form a soft dough. Cover with clingfilm and chill in the refrigerator for 15 minutes. Roll the pastry out on a floured work surface and use to line eight tartlet tins. Chill for 30 minutes.

2 Preheat the oven to 200°C/400°F/Gas Mark 6. Prick the bases of the cases, then line with baking paper and fill with baking beans. Bake blind in the preheated oven for 10 minutes, then remove the paper and beans and bake for a further 5–10 minutes, or until crisp and golden. Transfer the tins to a wire rack to cool. Reduce the oven temperature to 180°C/350°F/ Gas Mark 4.

3 Place the mascarpone, icing sugar and eggs in a bowl and whisk, then stir in the double cream. Remove the cases from the tins and place on a baking sheet. Fill each case with the mascarpone mix and bake for 10 minutes, or until starting to set. Leave to cool, then chill for 2 hours. Stone and halve the cherries, then arrange on the tarts. Melt the jam with the water in a saucepan, then drizzle over.

FRUIT COCKTAIL POPS

Makes: 8

Prep: 35 mins,
plus cooling & freezing

Cook: 6–8 mins

Ingredients

225 g/8 oz strawberries, hulled

2 small ripe peaches, peeled, stoned and roughly chopped (or 250 g/9 oz canned peaches, drained)

4 large kiwi fruits, peeled and roughly chopped

Sugar syrup

2 tbsp caster sugar

5 tbsp water

Method

1 To make the sugar syrup, put the sugar and water into a saucepan over a low heat and stir until the sugar has dissolved. Increase the heat until boiling, then simmer for 3–4 minutes. Remove the pan from the heat and leave the sugar syrup to cool completely before using.

2 Put the strawberries in a blender and whizz until puréed. Stir in 2 tablespoons of the sugar syrup. Pour the mixture into eight 125-ml/4 fl-oz ice pop moulds. Freeze for 2 hours or until firm.

3 When the strawberry mixture is frozen, put the peaches in the blender and whizz until puréed. Stir in half of the remaining sugar syrup. Pour the peach mixture over the frozen strawberry mixture. Insert the ice pop sticks and freeze for 2 hours, or until firm.

4 When the peach mixture is frozen, put the kiwi fruits in the blender and whizz until puréed. Stir in the remaining sugar syrup. Pour the kiwi mixture over the frozen peach mixture and freeze for 2 hours, or until firm.

5 To unmould the ice pops, dip the frozen moulds into warm water for a few seconds and gently release the pops while holding the sticks.

DESSERTS

CHOCOLATE ICE-CREAM BITES

Serves: 6

Prep: 25 mins,
plus freezing

Cook: 5 mins

Ingredients

600 ml/1 pint good-quality
vanilla ice cream

200 g/7 oz plain chocolate,
broken into pieces

2 tbsp unsalted butter

Method

1 Line a baking sheet with baking paper.

2 Using a melon baller, scoop out balls of ice
cream and place them on the prepared baking
sheet. Alternatively, cut the ice cream into
bite-sized cubes. Stick a cocktail stick in each
piece and return to the freezer until very hard.

3 Place the chocolate and the butter in a
heatproof bowl set over a saucepan of gently
simmering water until melted. Quickly dip the
frozen ice-cream balls into the warm chocolate
and return to the freezer. Keep them there until
ready to serve.

DESSERTS

SWEET PUMPKIN PIE

Serves: 8

Prep: 50 mins,
plus cooling & chilling

Cook: 2 hours 20 mins

Ingredients

1.8 kg/4 lb sweet pumpkin, halved and deseeded, stem and stringy bits removed

140 g/5 oz plain flour, plus extra for dusting

¼ tsp baking powder

1½ tsp ground cinnamon

¾ tsp ground nutmeg

¾ tsp ground cloves

1 tsp salt

50 g/1¾ oz caster sugar

55 g/2 oz cold unsalted butter, diced, plus extra for greasing

3 eggs

400 ml/14 fl oz canned condensed milk

½ tsp vanilla extract

1 tbsp demerara sugar

Streusel topping

2 tbsp plain flour

4 tbsp demerara sugar

1 tsp ground cinnamon

2 tbsp cold unsalted butter, diced

75 g/2¾ oz pecan nuts, chopped

75 g/2¾ oz walnuts, chopped

Method

1. Preheat the oven to 190°C/375°F/Gas Mark 5. Put the pumpkin halves, face down, in a shallow baking tin and cover with foil. Bake in the preheated oven for 1½ hours, then leave to cool. Scoop out the flesh and purée in a food processor. Drain off any excess liquid. Cover and chill.

2. Grease a 23-cm/9-inch round tart tin. To make the pastry, sift the flour and baking powder into a large bowl. Stir in ½ teaspoon of the cinnamon, ¼ teaspoon of the nutmeg, ¼ teaspoon of the cloves, ½ teaspoon of the salt and all the caster sugar. Rub in the butter with your fingertips until the mixture resembles fine breadcrumbs, then make a well in the centre. Lightly beat one of the eggs and pour it into the well. Mix together with a wooden spoon, then shape the dough into a ball. Place the dough on a lightly floured surface, roll out and use to line the prepared tin. Trim the edges, then cover and chill for 30 minutes.

3. Preheat the oven to 220°C/425°F/Gas Mark 7. Put the pumpkin purée in a large bowl, then stir in the condensed milk and the remaining eggs. Add the remaining spices and salt, then stir in the vanilla extract and demerara sugar. Pour into the pastry case and bake in the preheated oven for 15 minutes.

DESSERTS

4. Meanwhile, make the topping. Mix the flour, demerara sugar and cinnamon in a bowl, rub in the butter, then stir in the nuts. Remove the pie from the oven and reduce the heat to 180°C/350°F/Gas Mark 4. Sprinkle over the topping, then bake for a further 35 minutes. Remove from the oven and serve hot or cold.

BANANA CREAM PIE

Serves: 8–10

Prep: 35–40 mins, plus cooling & chilling

Cook: 25–30 mins

Ingredients

flour, for dusting

350 g/12 oz ready-made shortcrust pastry, thawed, if frozen

4 large egg yolks

85 g/3 oz caster sugar

4 tbsp cornflour

pinch of salt

450 ml/16 fl oz milk

1 tsp vanilla extract

3 bananas

½ tbsp lemon juice

350 ml/12 fl oz double cream, whipped with 3 tbsp icing sugar, to decorate

Method

1 Preheat the oven to 200°C/400°F/Gas Mark 6. Very lightly flour a rolling pin and use to roll out the pastry on a lightly floured work surface into a 30-cm/12-inch round. Line a 23-cm/9-inch pie dish with the pastry, then trim the excess pastry and prick the base all over with a fork. Line the pastry case with baking paper and fill with baking beans.

2 Bake blind in the preheated oven for 15 minutes, or until the pastry is a light golden colour. Remove the paper and beans and prick the base again. Return to the oven and bake for a further 5–10 minutes, until golden and dry. Leave to cool completely on a wire rack.

3 Meanwhile, put the egg yolks, sugar, cornflour and salt into a bowl and beat until blended and pale in colour. Beat in the milk and vanilla extract.

4 Pour the mixture into a heavy-based saucepan over a medium–high heat and bring to the boil, stirring, until smooth and thick. Reduce the heat to low and simmer, stirring, for 2 minutes. Strain the mixture into a bowl and set aside to cool.

5 Slice the bananas, place in a bowl with the lemon juice and toss. Arrange them in the cooled pastry case, then top with the custard and chill in the refrigerator for at least 2 hours. Spread the cream over the top of the pie and serve.

MANGO & PASSION FRUIT FOOL

Serves: 4   **Prep: 20–25 mins**   **Cook: No cooking**

Ingredients

1 mango
2 passion fruit
40 g/1½ oz caster sugar
4 tbsp vegetarian white wine
300 ml/10 fl oz double cream

Method

1 Halve, stone and thinly peel the mango. Place the flesh in a food processor or blender and whizz to a smooth purée.

2 Scoop out the flesh from the passion fruit and add half to the mango purée.

3 Put the sugar, wine and cream into a bowl and whip until it holds its shape.

4 Fold the fruit purée lightly into the cream, then spoon into four serving bowls.

5 Spoon the remaining passion fruit on top of each and serve.

★ Variation

For an extra-special treat, add some white chocolate shavings over the top of each fool.

INDEX

apples
 Apple & Blackberry Crumble 230
 Caramelized Apple & Blue Cheese
  Salad 31
 Sweet Potato & Apple Soup 16
Asparagus & Pea Frittata 66
aubergines
 Baked Aubergine with Tomato Sauce 140
 Grilled Aubergines with Red Pepper, Feta
  & Mint 82
 Melting Mozzarella Bagels 78
 Quinoa-Stuffed Aubergines 180
 Ratatouille & Potato Wedges 138
 Spicy Vegetable Lasagne 112
 Tofu Moussaka 200-201
 Vegetable Chilli 122
 Vegetarian Paella 202
avocados
 Chilli Tofu Tortillas 126-127
 Chunky Avocado & Sweetcorn Salad 46

Banana Cream Pie 250-251
beans
 Baby Squash with Freekeh Stuffing 169
 Bean & Tomato Casserole with Parmesan
  Toasts 154
 Borlotti Bean, Tomato & Onion Salad with
  Eggs 34
 Hoppin' John 131
 Kale & Butter Bean Casserole 194-195
 Roast Butternut Squash 150
 Spring Stew 114
 Vegetable Chilli 122
 Vegetarian Chilli Burgers 108
 Vegetarian Hot Dogs 116
 Vegetarian Paella 202
beansprouts
 Classic Stir-fried Vegetables 90
 Gado Gado Salad 40
beetroot
 Beetroot & Roquefort Wraps 80
 Broccoli Salad 42
 Radicchio & Red Pepper Salad 54
 Raw Beetroot & Pecan Salad 47
 Roast Beetroot Parcels with Horseradish
  Butter 198-199
broad beans
 Bruschetta With Broad Beans, Mint &
  Goat's Cheese 72
 Spring Stew 114
 Vegetable Pie 119
broccoli
 Broccoli & Stilton Soup 19
 Broccoli Salad 42
 Chilli Broccoli Pasta 98
 Classic Stir-fried Vegetables 90
 Gado Gado Salad 40
 Kale Stir-Fry 94
 Sprouting Broccoli with Caper Butter
  Sauce 186
 Sweet Potato & Halloumi Burgers 120
 Vegetable Pie 119

cabbage
 Broccoli Salad 42
 Classic Stir-fried Vegetables 90
 Gado Gado Salad 40
 Red Cabbage Stuffed with Mushrooms,
  Nuts & Rice 192-193

 Spring Cabbage & Radish Slaw with
  Pumpkin Seeds 36
 Spring Stew 114
carrots
 Carrot & Coriander Sausages &
  Mash 110-111
 Carrot & Coriander Soup 10
 Carrot & Orange Stir-Fry 60
 Carrot, Coconut & Mango Salad 38
 Carrot Tarte Tatin 168
 Chunky Vegetable Soup 29
 Roasted Root Soup with Ginger &
  Crème Fraîche 26-27
 Spring Stew 114
 Vegetable Pie 119
cauliflower
 Cauliflower Cheese 100
 Gado Gado Salad 40
 Potato & Radish Salad 48-49
celery & celeriac
 Celeriac Soup with Cheese Pastry
  Sticks 12-13
 Pear, Celery, Blue Cheese & Walnut
  Salad 32
 Roasted Squash & Celeriac with
  Balsamic Glaze 181
chard
 Chard & Ricotta Filo Pie 176-177
 Rainbow Salad with Wasabi Dressing 50
cheese
 Bean & Tomato Casserole with Parmesan
  Toasts 154
 Beetroot & Roquefort Wraps 80
 Broccoli & Stilton Soup 19
 Bruschetta with Broad Beans, Mint &
  Goat's Cheese 72
 Caramelized Apple & Blue Cheese
  Salad 31
 Cauliflower Cheese 100
 Chard & Ricotta Filo Pie 176-177
 Griddled Courgette & Feta Pizza 144-145
 Grilled Aubergines with Red Pepper,
  Feta & Mint 82
 Leek & Goat's Cheese Crêpes 79
 Leek & Goat's Cheese Tartlets 74
 Macaroni Cheese 104
 Melting Mozzarella Bagels 78
 New Potato, Feta & Herb Frittata 146
 New York Cheesecake 226-227
 Pear, Celery, Blue Cheese & Walnut
  Salad 32
 Penne in Tomato Sauce with Two
  Cheeses 152
 Poached Eggs 'Florentine' with Spinach
  & Cheddar 62
 Portobello Mushroom Burgers with
  Mozzarella 86
 Pumpkin & Gruyère Stew 179
 Soufflé Jacket Potatoes 128
 Spinach & Ricotta Cannelloni 142-143
 Strawberry Cheesecake 214
 Sweet Potato & Halloumi Burgers 120
 Tomato, Olive & Mozzarella Pasta Salad 52
cherries
 Fresh Black Cherry Pies 244
 Latticed Cherry Pie 210-211
chickpeas
 Falafel Burgers 92
 Moroccan Vegetables 182

 Squash, Kale & Farro Stew 204
chocolate
 Cappuccino Soufflés 240
 Chocolate Ice-Cream Bites 247
 Chocolate Mousse 212
 Ice-Cream Brownie Sundae 236
 Raspberry & White Chocolate Brûlées 232
 Rich Chocolate Tarts 228
 Toffee Chocolate Puff Tarts 238
courgettes
 Chunky Vegetable Soup 29
 Courgette & Basil Risotto 197
 Griddled Courgette & Feta Pizza 144-145
 Griddled Courgette, Pepper & Tomato Gratin 134
 Moroccan Vegetables 182
 Rigatoni with Roast Courgette &
  Tomato Sauce 148
 Vegetable Chilli 122
 Watercress, Courgette & Mint Salad 30
couscous
 Couscous with Roast Cherry Tomatoes
  & Pine Nuts 81
 Moroccan Vegetables 182
Crème Brûlée 231
cucumbers
 Gado Gado Salad 40
 Yellow Tomato Gazpacho 22

eggs
 Asparagus & Pea Frittata 66
 Borlotti Bean, Tomato & Onion Salad
  with Eggs 34
 Eggs with Fried Tomato, Onions &
  Peppers 103
 New Potato, Feta & Herb Frittata 146
 Poached Eggs 'Florentine' with Spinach
  & Cheddar 62
 Wild Mushroom Omelette 88

Fennel Risotto with Vodka 172
Fig & Watermelon Salad 219
French beans
 Potato & Radish Salad 48-49
 Vegetarian Paella 202
 Watercress, Courgette & Mint Salad 30
Fruit Cocktail Pops 246

Jerusalem Artichoke & Hazelnut Gratin 160

kale
 Kale & Butter Bean Casserole 194-195
 Kale Stir-Fry 94
 Squash, Kale & Farro Stew 204
Key Lime Pie 220

leeks
 Carrot & Orange Stir-Fry 60
 Leek & Goat's Cheese Crêpes 79
 Leek & Goat's Cheese Tartlets 74
 Leek & Potato Soup 28
 Leek & Spinach Soup 8
Lemon Meringue Pie 224-225
lentils
 Lentil Bolognese 124
 Sweet Potato Curry with Lentils 118

mangoes
 Carrot, Coconut & Mango Salad 38
 Mango & Passion Fruit Fool 252

mushrooms
Classic Stir-fried Vegetables 90
Cream of Mushroom Soup 18
Creamed Morels on Spinach & Polenta Croûtons 164-165
Fettuccine with Tomato & Mushroom Sauce 70
Layered Potato & Mushroom Pie 130
Mushroom & Tofu Laksa with Noodles 24
Mushroom & Walnut Open Tart 178
Mushroom Stroganoff 76
Mushrooms & Sizzled Sage on Sourdough Toast 68
Portabello Mushroom Burgers with Mozzarella 86
Red Cabbage Stuffed with Mushrooms, Nuts & Rice 192-193
Roast Butternut Squash 150
Spicy Vegetable Lasagne 112
Vegetarian Paella 202
Warm Butternut Squash, Mushroom & Spinach Salad 44-45
Wild Mushroom Omelette 88
Wild Mushroom Risotto 174

nuts
Baby Squash with Freekeh Stuffing 169
Broccoli with Peanuts 102
Carrot & Coriander Sausages & Mash 110-111
Carrot, Coconut & Mango Salad 38
Gado Gado Salad 40
Jerusalem Artichoke & Hazelnut Gratin 160
Mixed Nut Roast with Cranberry & Red Wine Sauce 166
Mushroom & Walnut Open Tart 178
Pear, Celery, Blue Cheese & Walnut Salad 32
Potato Gnocchi with Walnut Pesto 184-185
Pumpkin & Chestnut Risotto 188-189
Quinoa-Stuffed Aubergines 180
Raw Beetroot & Pecan Salad 47
Red Cabbage Stuffed with Mushrooms, Nuts & Rice 192-193
Sticky Coffee & Walnut Sponges 242

Onion Tart, Caramelized 196

parsnips
Parsnip Layered Casserole 147
Spiced Parsnip Gratin with Ginger Cream 158

pasta
Baked Gnocchi with Tomato Sauce 162-163
Chilli Broccoli Pasta 98
Fettuccine with Tomato & Mushroom Sauce 70
Lentil Bolognese 124
Macaroni Cheese 129
Pasta Pesto 64
Penne in Tomato Sauce with Two Cheeses 152
Potato Gnocchi with Walnut Pesto 184-185
Rigatoni with Roast Courgette & Tomato Sauce 148
Spaghetti Olio e Aglio 104
Spicy Vegetable Lasagne 112
Spinach & Ricotta Cannelloni 142-143
Sweet Potato Ravioli with Sage Butter 132-133

Tomato, Olive & Mozzarella Pasta Salad 52
Peach Cobbler 218
Pear, Celery, Blue Cheese & Walnut Salad 32
peas
Asparagus & Pea Frittata 66
Easy Rice & Peas 84
Pea & Herb Soup with Basil Oil 20
peppers
Chilli Tofu Tortillas 126-127
Courgette, Pepper & Tomato Gratin 134
Eggs with Fried Tomato, Onions & Peppers 103
Grilled Aubergines with Red Pepper, Feta & Mint 82
Kale Stir-Fry 94
Radicchio & Red Pepper Salad 54
Ratatouille & Potato Wedges 138
Spicy Vegetable Lasagne 112
Sweetcorn, Chilli & Tortilla Gratin 170-171
Vegetable Chilli 122
Vegetarian Paella 202
potatoes
Carrot & Coriander Sausages & Mash 110-111
Layered Potato & Mushroom Pie 130
Leek & Potato Soup 8
Leek & Spinach Soup 8
New Potato, Feta & Herb Frittata 146
New Potato, Rosemary & Rocket Pizza 58
Potato & Radish Salad 48-49
Potato Gnocchi with Walnut Pesto 184-185
Ratatouille & Potato Wedges 138
Soufflé Jacket Potatoes 128
Spring Stew 114
Tofu Moussaka 200-201
pumpkin & squash
Baby Squash with Freekeh Stuffing 169
Pumpkin & Chestnut Risotto 188-189
Pumpkin & Gruyère Stew 179
Roast Butternut Squash 150
Roasted Squash & Celeriac with Balsamic Glaze 181
Squash, Kale & Farro Stew 204
Sweet Pumpkin Pie 248-249
Warm Butternut Squash, Mushroom & Spinach Salad 44-45

Quinoa-Stuffed Aubergines 180

radishes
Potato & Radish Salad 48-49
Radicchio & Red Pepper Salad 54
Raw Beetroot & Pecan Salad 47
Spring Cabbage & Radish Slaw with Pumpkin Seeds 36
Raspberry & White Chocolate Brûlées 232
Red Wine Sorbet 229
rice
Courgette & Basil Risotto 197
Easy Rice & Peas 84
Fennel Risotto with Vodka 172
Hoppin' John 131
Pumpkin & Chestnut Risotto 188-189
Red Cabbage Stuffed with Mushrooms, Nuts & Rice 192-193
Rice Pudding 208
Stuffed Tomatoes 69
Vegetarian Paella 202
Wild Mushroom Risotto 174

Salted Caramel Pies 222

spinach
Creamed Morels on Spinach & Polenta Croûtons 164-165
Leek & Spinach Soup 8
Macaroni Cheese 129
New Potato, Feta & Herb Frittata 146
Poached Eggs 'Florentine' with Spinach & Cheddar 62
Potato & Radish Salad 48-49
Spinach & Ricotta Cannelloni 142-143
Warm Butternut Squash, Mushroom & Spinach Salad 44-45
strawberries
Eton Mess 216
Strawberry Cheesecake 214
Summer Pavlova 234
sweet potatoes
Roasted Root Soup with Ginger & Crème Fraîche 26-27
Sweet Potato & Apple Soup 16
Sweet Potato & Halloumi Burgers 120
Sweet Potato Curry with Lentils 118
Sweet Potato Ravioli with Sage Butter 132-133
sweetcorn
Chunky Avocado & Sweetcorn Salad 46
Classic Stir-fried Vegetables 90
Spring Stew 114
Sweetcorn, Chilli & Tortilla Gratin 170-171
Vegetable Pie 119

tofu
Chilli Tofu Tortillas 126-127
Mushroom & Tofu Laksa with Noodles 24
Thai Tofu Cakes with Chilli Dip 136
Tofu Moussaka 200-201
Tofu Parcels 96
tomatoes
Baked Aubergine with Tomato Sauce 140
Baked Gnocchi with Tomato Sauce 162-163
Bean & Tomato Casserole with Parmesan Toasts 154
Borlotti Bean, Tomato & Onion Salad with Eggs 34
Courgette, Pepper & Tomato Gratin 134
Couscous with Roast Cherry Tomatoes & Pine Nuts 81
Eggs with Fried Tomato, Onions & Peppers 103
Fettuccine with Tomato & Mushroom Sauce 70
Hoppin' John 131
Lentil Bolognese 124
Parsnip Layered Casserole 147
Penne in Tomato Sauce with Two Cheeses 152
Rigatoni with Roast Courgette & Tomato Sauce 148
Stuffed Tomatoes 69
Sweetcorn, Chilli & Tortilla Gratin 170-171
Tofu Moussaka 200-201
Tomato, Olive & Mozzarella Pasta Salad 52
Tomato Soufflé 190-191
Tomato Soup 14
Vegetable Chilli 122
Vegetarian Paella 202
Yellow Tomato Gazpacho 22

Watercress, Courgette & Mint Salad 30

INDEX

This edition published by Parragon Books Ltd in 2015
LOVE FOOD is an imprint of Parragon Books Ltd

Parragon Books Ltd
Chartist House
15–17 Trim Street
Bath BA1 1HA, UK
www.parragon.com/lovefood

Copyright © Parragon Books Ltd 2014-2015

LOVE FOOD and the accompanying heart device is a registered
trademark of Parragon Books Ltd in Australia, the UK, USA, India and the
EU.

ISBN 978-1-4723-6464-7
Printed in China

Cover photography by Ian Garlick
Introduction by Anne Sheasby

Notes for the Reader
This book uses both metric and imperial measurements. Follow the
same units of measurement throughout; do not mix metric and imperial.
All spoon measurements are level: teaspoons are assumed to be 5 ml,
and tablespoons are assumed to be 15 ml. Unless otherwise stated, milk
is assumed to be full fat, eggs and individual vegetables are medium,
and pepper is freshly ground black pepper. Unless otherwise stated, all
root vegetables should be peeled prior to using.

Garnishes, decorations and serving suggestions are all optional and
not necessarily included in the recipe ingredients or method. The
times given are an approximate guide only. Preparation times differ
according to the techniques used by different people and the cooking
times may also vary from those given. Optional ingredients, variations or
serving suggestions have not been included in the time calculations.

Vegetarians should be aware that some of the ready-made ingredients
used in the recipes in this book may contain animal products. Always
check the packaging before use.